FC3095.D84 R67 2003

Ross, Nicola, 1957-

Dufferin County /

[2003]

0 1341 0731942 5

Dufferin County

Nicola Ross with photography by Rosemary Hasner

A BOSTON MILLS PRESS BOOK

National Library of Canada Cataloguing in Publication

Ross, Nicola, 1957-

Dufferin County / Nicola Ross ; with photography by Rosemary Hasner.
Includes bibliographical references and index.

ISBN 1-55046-413-2
1. Dufferin (Ont. : County)—History. I. Hasner, Rosemary II. Title.
FC3095.D8R68 2003   971.3'41   C2003-901174-7   F1059.D88R68 2003

Published by BOSTON MILLS PRESS
132 Main Street, Erin, Ontario, Canada N0B 1T0
Tel 519-833-2407   Fax 519-833-2195
e-mail: books@bostonmillspress.com   www.bostonmillspress.com

In Canada: Distributed by Firefly Books Ltd.
3680 Victoria Park Avenue, Toronto, Ontario, Canada M2H 3K1

In the United States: Distributed by Firefly Books (U.S.) Inc.
P.O. Box 1338, Ellicott Station, Buffalo, New York, USA 14205

Design: McCorkindale Advertising & Design

Printed in Singapore

The publisher acknowledges the financial support of the Government of Canada through the
Book Publishing Industry Development Program (BPIDP), for its publishing efforts.

JACKET:
Top right: Shelly Anderson's century home on Airport Road. Top middle: Farm fiels, Mulmur.
Top left: A lush carpet of green covers the forest floor in the Boyne Valley Provincial Park.
Bottom: The Pine River is famous for its trout and salmon runs.

REAR JACKET: Energy from the wind.

Page 1: Dufferin's many watercourses rise and fall as they cross the Niagara Escarpment.
Mrs. Fennell's falls is one of a number of waterfalls in the county.
Page 2: Early morning mist.
Page 3: Murphy's Pinnacle in Mulmur.

Contents

Foreword   7

Acknowledgments   8

Introduction   10

Chapter One: A Rich and Natural History   18

Chapter Two: Up in Orange Country   34

Chapter Three: Rails, Trails, But No Highwaymen   48

Chapter Four: Dufferin's Laborious Birth   64

Chapter Five: Still the Mainstay of Dufferin's Economy   82

Chapter Six: A Hotbed of Culture   104

Chapter Seven: The Hollow at Horning's Mills   118

In Conclusion   130

Bibliography   134

Index of Place Names   136

The Pine River.

Foreword

I've spent a lifetime farming in Dufferin County, enjoying a close association with the soil, in the production of livestock and the planting and harvesting of agricultural and forest crops. This life has given me the opportunity to appreciate farming practices first hand, especially as they relate to land stewardship. Now, as pressure from urban development is increasing, the conservation and preservation of our beautiful county is of utmost importance.

Over the years the landscape has changed dramatically. To me, the most significant change is the increased forest cover that we have today. Compare it with 1909, the year I was born. Back then, because so much land had been cleared to make way for farmers' ploughs, trees covered only about 20 percent of Mono Township. Since then, we've learned a great deal about the land and should apply what we know so we can avoid making mistakes.

An outstanding example of the need for trees is a piece of land on the east half of Lot 13 on Mono's Sixth Concession (on Airport Road just north of the Hockley Road). Because the trees had been cut down to make way for farming, sand was drifting out on to the roadway. Sand dunes could be six feet deep. So the landowner gave the township permission to plant trees on his property. Now you can scarcely find the old sand dunes among the towering pine trees, but I remember when a horse-drawn grader cleared the road so cars could get through.

The forest cover in our county has more than doubled due to the government's reforestation program. The province supplied the seedlings free of charge, and school groups, Scouts and Guides, service clubs and private landowners undertook springtime tree plantings. As the program progressed so did enthusiasm, particularly among private landowners. Today there are several hundred acres of County Forest and Forest Tracts in many townships. We've learned that we can work with Mother Nature to protect our environment.

As suitable habitat increased, native animal species returned. Beaver and white-tailed deer reappeared. Early settlers reported that huge flocks of passenger pigeons "darkened the sky." Sadly, these amazing birds were last sighted in 1914 and are now extinct, but many other birds can now find homes in Dufferin's forests. The Eastern bluebird, adored by bird lovers everywhere, is a wonderful example. By 1940, it was on the endangered species list. Yet, in 2001, a local birder banded over 500 fledgling bluebirds.

The success story of the return of the forest in Dufferin County is gratifying and inspirational. Such results could not have been achieved without the help of the dedicated and concerned people of the area. This is just one of the stories of Dufferin County. The historical record can provide exciting reading. It is also a valuable source of information. Today's stories are equally inspirational. The writer of this book, Nicola Ross, and Rosemary Hasner, the photographer, are a dedicated pair with a passion for conservation and restoration. I congratulate them on the time, effort and thought that went into this book.

— *Sheldon Anderson, Town of Mono, August 2002*

Acknowledgments

It's taken me long months of research, meetings, discussions and getting lost on back roads to get to know Dufferin County. I've had people take me to their favourite places. Others have told me about their lives and loves. I've perused dozens of family diaries, church histories and old newspapers. People have read my words, suggested improvements, corrections and additions. Without fail, everyone has been kind, generous and enthusiastic. They've happily given me their time, their ideas and thoughts. I thank everyone who is part of this book. You, your neighbours and the dramatic landscape are the soul of Dufferin County.

In particular, I'd like to acknowledge those who've gone an extra mile to help out: Bruce Beach, Robert Bell, Ellen Bryan, Earl Dodds, Norma Gallaugher, Jennifer Grant, Isabel and John Ireland, Marjorie Milroy, Shirley Orr, Terry Sullivan, Walter Tovell, Gordon Townsend, Bert and Patricia Tupling, Jean Turnbull and all the people who have written church and community histories and donated them to the Dufferin County Museum and Archives.

Then there are a few individuals who came through time and again. An extra special thanks to Shelly Anderson, an inspiration to all conservationists; Signe Ball, who actually feels the community; Steve Brown, who simply knows everything and painstakingly reviewed each chapter word by word; and Wayne Townsend, who just is Dufferin County. And you guys at Boston Mills Press did it again. John Denison, Kathy Fraser, and Noel Hudson, you make our words and photos look so good. Thanks also to designers Sue Breen and Chris McCorkindale.

Finally, thank you Rosemary Hasner and Janet Eagleson for capturing Dufferin County with your camera and your Dufferin County spirit.

— *Nicola Ross*

Author's note: Dufferin County wasn't formed until 1881. This made it difficult to write the text since there are times when I refer to things happening in Dufferin County before it actually existed. For example, I might say that early settlers passed Dufferin County by, when, in fact, it had not yet been formed. I hope you will excuse this inconsistency in the writing, knowing that it's the only situation where accuracy knowingly gave way to efficiency.

To Neil, my partner.
I've learned so much from you. Thank you for
always listening to my hare-brained ideas…
and sometimes taking them seriously.

A windy spot high above Mansfield.

J ust over four years ago, I bought an old school house on the easternmost edge of Dufferin. It was a moment that changed my life. I've fallen in love with the countryside, the people and the land. This book was a labour of love — I hope my passion for this wonderful place comes through on each and every page.

So many people helped me with this book. My deepest thanks go to author and project partner Nicola Ross, and to Debbie Baker and the Camilla United Church Women, Julie Baumlisberger, Bruce Beach, the Besley boys, Mary Cornfield, Bill French, Linda Jenetti, Susan Loewen, Al Pace, Dave Raynor, Pam and Russell Stewart, Wayne Townsend and Lin Ward for their time and enthusiasm. Special thanks to the folks at Boston Mills Press — John Denison, for his unflagging support, and Sue Breen and Chris McCorkindale, for their incredible design talent.

Sometimes, words aren't enough to say thank you. The irrepressible Shelly Anderson started as a photo subject and became a friend. Shelly, you've changed my perspective on so many things. Thank you. Phyllis McDowell, who shared her home, her music, her friendship and her knowledge with me — thanks, Phyl. I can't wait until next year's après-fiddle hoedown. And Janet Eagleson, who helped me in so many ways I don't know where to begin. Navigator, negotiator, photo assistant, manager, secretary and supreme coffeemaker — these photos wouldn't be what they are without you. Thank you.

—*Rosemary Hasner*

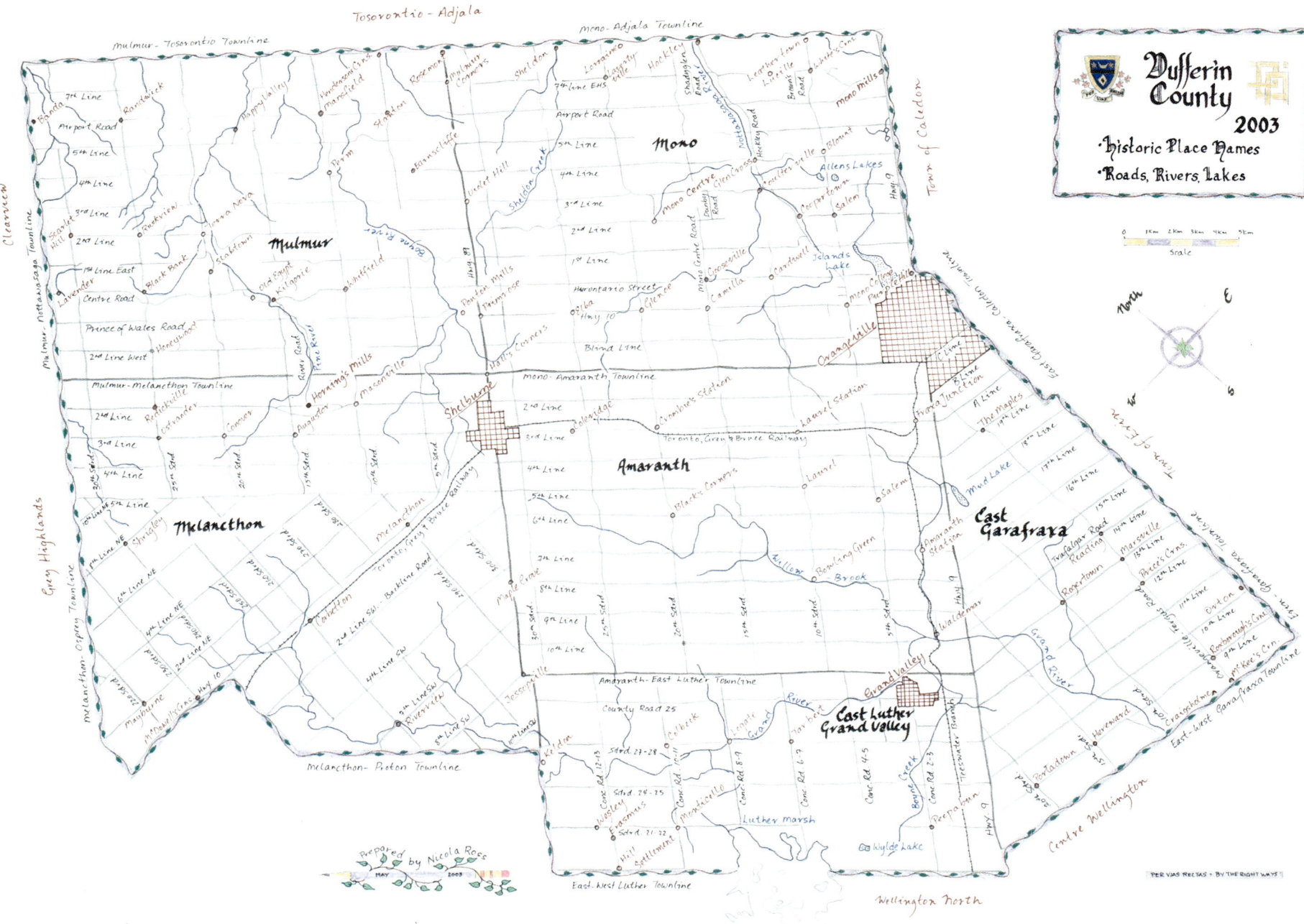

Introduction

"Dufferin County is this hidden gem in Ontario's heartland. It's the rolling green hills in spring and summer. It's the mature beech, oak and maple trees in splendid fall colours. It's the crisp clear winter days when the only sound is the whisper of your skis on the snow. It is people who are as connected with their rural past as they are to maintaining the countryside today. It's my home."
— *Bernadette Hardaker, resident of Orangeville.*

"I've learned to like it. I wasn't sure I would, but I did."
— *Mary Lazier, potter, lives on land in Violet Hill inherited from her mother.*

Ask a dozen people from Dufferin County where they live and they will specify Mono or Shelburne, Orangeville or Melancthon. If they've been in the Hockley Valley long enough, they might say they're from the "Huckley," but "Dufferin County" passes few lips.

I suppose this shouldn't be a surprise. After all, I would never describe my home as Peel Region even though I grew up in Caledon Township and reside in the hamlet of Belfountain. But somehow it's different in Dufferin County. There's something about the pride in people's voices when they respond to my query, something about the pinpoint precision of their response—a woman from Camilla told me she lives in a suburb of Gooseville—that makes it sound as if residents delight in avoiding the term Dufferin County.

So I investigated this idiosyncrasy and discovered that even though it came together as a county over 120 years ago, the borders separating Dufferin's towns and townships have not disappeared. Dufferin is, and maybe always will be, a collection of villagers, townspeople and rural folk who co-exist in their communities in relative harmony…most of the time. When challenged, citizens of Dufferin County haven't always pulled together to

Corbetton, looking east, circa 1900. The church is now on the grounds of the Dufferin County Museum and Archives.

"battle the foe." Instead, such events have accentuated the differences among communities, and between rural and urban interests. This fierce protection of local values, it turns out, goes back a long way, all the way, in fact, to Dufferin's very beginnings.

Before Dufferin, Ontario's youngest and smallest county, was finally formed in 1881, its towns and townships were affiliated with well-established counties: Melancthon and Shelburne were part of Grey County; Luther, East Garafraxa, Amaranth and Orangeville hailed from Wellington; and both Mono and Mulmur were in Simcoe.

But Orangeville had grand aspirations. Since it would become the seat of government in a new county, this ambitious town had much to gain by leaving Wellington County. Urged on by town elders, residents voted 572 to 2 for the new union. The northern townships, by contrast, didn't share Orangeville's enthusiasm. People living in Mulmur voted 635 to 1 against making a move, while those who supported amalgamation in Melancthon

Mono Centre, looking east, circa 1890.

were outnumbered by a margin of 435 to 57. And centrally located Shelburne, jealous of Orangeville's rising star, also voted against joining forces.

Given this history, it's no wonder that even though there is no one alive today who was around back in 1881, residents remain loyal to their village, town or township. This characteristic remained clearly evident more than a century later, in 1999. That year, what can only be described as a furor erupted when, at the provincial government's bidding, politicians in Orangeville and Shelburne put forward a proposal to tear down the borders between townships and convert the county into a seamless, modern-day City of Dufferin.

Compounding citizens' concerns that the proposal meant they would have to give up their towns and townships was a clash between rural and urban values. While Dufferin's warden, at the time, promoted a new governance model that fostered a change from the county's historical rural, agricultural-based economy to a more urban, industrial-based one, Mono's mayor countered by championing local values. He dismissed the City of Dufferin model because it failed to recognize the differences between communities. In the end, the provincial government backed off on its push to have municipalities haul down their internal borders, and Dufferin's restructuring battle subsided. But the event illustrated that respecting local values was more important than promises of economic gain achieved though homogenization. After the next municipal election, Mono's pro-local mayor became Dufferin's warden.

Throughout its history, agriculture has been the mainstay of Dufferin's economy. Once its marketable trees had been cut down, and after concrete and bricks diminished the demand for the sandstone quarried in the Hockley Valley, only agriculture remained.

Today, agriculture is still Dufferin's largest economic sector. But the farmers that inspired author Dan Needles to poke fun at the relations between old timers and incoming city folk in his Wingfield series of plays are a disappearing breed in Dufferin County. The 100- or 200-acre mixed farm run by a husband, wife, their kids and a couple of hired hands has given way to some new forms of agriculture.

Many farms, especially in Mono and Mulmur where the rocky soil makes farming difficult, have been sold to weekenders who might lease the land back to the farmer. But they might also turn them into horse farms or re-establish the forests that once characterized the landscape. At the same time, especially in Dufferin's best agricultural area, where one finds prized Honeywood silt loam, agri-business has replaced mixed farming. If you have any doubts about this agricultural trend, visit a potato farm north of Shelburne and witness a $300,000, climate-controlled building where over five million spuds can be stored, or look across a feedlot that handles 1,000 or more cattle. Alternatively, some farmers are returning to the age-old practice of farm-gate sales. They're finding that selling vegetables, chicken, beef and fruit pies directly to customers supplements their other farm income quite nicely.

Orangeville has matured into a vibrant town. Young families fill its neighbourhoods. Its residents frequent interesting restaurants, athletic facilities, parks and playgrounds. The light manufacturing plants that now fill the industrial lands on the outskirts of town provide much-needed jobs. The farmers' market that takes place each Saturday morning from May through October sets up behind the Opera House on Broadway at the same spot that farmers visited almost 100 years ago to buy cattle.

Redickville, circa 1900.

Dufferin today is a richly textured community of communities. Alongside farmers, weekenders from Bay Street and young urban families, thrive citizens with an amazing array of talents and interests.

The number and quality of artists who are inspired by the high hills and have made them home is amazing. Jim Lorriman, for example, is an accomplished wood turner. Some of the wood he uses comes from the trees that grow on his Mulmur property. With it he crafts polished bowls so beautiful it's impossible to resist picking them up to study the grain and stroke the silky finish. Theatre and music abound. If Theatre Orangeville isn't performing in the Opera House on Broadway, it may have a jazz, classical or folk concert in progress. A glance at any back issue of *In the Hills* magazine attests to the depth of interesting and talented people who've settled in and around the high county.

And anyone who believes Dufferin County is a backward place populated by parochial-minded folk has to reconsider their point of view after visiting the Dufferin County Museum and Archives. While communities reputed to be more sophisticated and worldly continue

Monticello General Store, 1940s.

to convert historic buildings into community archives and museums only to find they are too small and not well suited to the purpose, Dufferin built a brand spanking new, 26,000-square-foot, fully climate-controlled "barn" and put the historic buildings inside. The contrast between the size and scope of this amazing facility and Dufferin's down-home reputation is the kind of stuff that has made Dan Needles' Wingfield series so engaging.

So too has Orangeville's decision to buy a railway. Purchased to give industrial businesses in Orangeville a competitive advantage, the Orangeville–Brampton Railway might one day shuttle theatre-goers from Toronto and Mississauga up to Orangeville for dinner and a play.

Just as the mighty Niagara Escarpment lies mostly buried and hidden in the high county, Dufferin's attributes may not be immediately obvious to a visitor or a newcomer. But the longer you farm, paint, manufacture or simply live in Dufferin County, the more you become aware of its secrets. And just as the mighty Niagara Escarpment, when it does appear, rises with dramatic effect, Dufferin's character, when you get to know it, is bold and intense.

William Thorsell, a weekender in Mulmur, president and CEO of the Royal Ontario Museum, writes: "Dufferin County has a wildness to it that marks a distinct change from Toronto's sphere of influence. You see and feel the difference immediately north of Highway 9, where the landscape is written more boldly, the weather is more beautifully violent, the hills rise more powerfully and the evidence of pioneer settlement is more clear. You can still get lost in Dufferin County, and be intimidated by the land and sky. Nature balances humanity more evenly there, and commands and keeps our attention."

However you find it, Dufferin County has stories worthy of its landscape. I hope you enjoy reading the stories about Dufferin County as much as I enjoyed researching and writing them. With my words and Rosemary Hasner's photographs, we have tried to capture the wonders, the character and the spirit of Dufferin's high hills.

With its deep valleys and soaring vistas, Mulmur seems close to the top of the world.

CHAPTER ONE

A Rich and Natural History

"Since I bought my place in 1978 I have become a full-time wood turner and have found that this land that was clear cut in the late 1800s has completely grown back and contains every specie of tree that is indigenous to Dufferin County. I need never leave! It doesn't get much better than this!"
—*Jim Lorriman, 53 years old, wood turner, community activist, Mulmur.*

"The Niagara Escarpment reflects about 500 million years of geological history. Surely that's worth studying and preserving. I've been visiting the Niagara Escarpment forever. It was a delight for my wife and me to end up living so close to it."
—*Walter Tovell, age 85, geologist and author of* Guide to the Geology of the Niagara Escarpment, *Mono.*

Take a drive through the Forks of the Credit, past Milton or up the Bruce Peninsula and you'll understand why there is so much fuss about protecting the Niagara Escarpment. In these places, its magnificent cliffs dominate the view. But in Dufferin, the Niagara Escarpment is a buried treasure. Extending the entire length of the county, from Mono Mills in the south to Lavender in the north, it peeks through in remarkably few places and only shows off in Mono Cliffs Provincial Park near Mono Centre.

The Niagara Escarpment is a cuesta, from the Spanish word meaning flank or slope. Composed of gently dipping rock strata with a long, gradual slope on one side and a relatively steep scarp on the other, Canada's 725-kilometre portion of the Niagara Escarpment extends from Niagara Falls in the south to the tip of Manitoulin Island. Geologists always note that erosion helped shape the Niagara Escarpment. It's also interesting to know that the Escarpment comprises rock that is as much as 450 million years old, that it is not a fault, and that it pre-dates the glaciers.

Evidence of the Niagara Escarpment can be spied along the Hockley Road, County Road 17 west of Mansfield and Mono Centre Road. Red outcroppings of Queenston shale, a soft layer of clay that underlies the entire Niagara Escarpment, line portions of these

Boyne Valley Provincial Park.

thoroughfares. A chemical reaction that causes a red iron mineral to turn grey accounts for the characteristic grey-green stripes.

Though the escarpment is mostly buried, quarrymen were not fooled. Tipped off by the Queenston shale outcroppings, they dug down through the gravel. Huge slabs of silver-grey limestone rewarded their sleuthing. They exploited this resource in the Owen Sound and Nicholson quarries. Located just north of the Hockley Road near Hurontario Street, these quarries were major operations around the turn of the last century. But as cement and other building materials entered the marketplace in the early 1900s, demand for limestone diminished until the quarries closed permanently in the 1920s.

Shirley Manor, constructed of materials from the Nicholson farm and quarry.

Limestone from these sites can be found in Toronto's old City Hall and inside Ontario's Parliament buildings at Queen's Park. The Exhibition Buildings at Exhibition Place feature limestone from Dufferin and dozens of Dufferin's century brick homes have cornerstones, sills and doorsteps quarried locally.

One of the best local examples of Dufferin's limestone is a house built by George Nicholson, the owner of the Nicholson Quarry. His showcase home, renamed Shirley Manor by his son-in-law, Arthur Shirley, is easy to pick out on the south side of the Hockley Road. Made entirely from local materials, this magnificent structure stands out as something special.

To understand why the escarpment is seldom evident in Dufferin, it's necessary to know something about the dirtier side of glaciers. Although they are thought of as pure ice, glaciers accumulate massive amounts of sand and gravel. One only has to imagine the muck that coats the ground each spring after the snow disappears to picture the amount of debris that remained after kilometre-thick glaciers melted some 12,000 to 13,000 years ago. As they receded, the glaciers deposited sand and gravel, which formed moraines and eskers. This accounts for the apparent absence of the Niagara Escarpment in Dufferin County. It is buried.

And nowhere along the escarpment's entire 725-kilometre length is it more completely covered up than near Highway 89 between Primrose and Violet Hill. Here the Orangeville Moraine totally masks the Niagara Escarpment's presence. Smaller than the better-known Oak Ridges Moraine, the Orangeville Moraine is nonetheless a major landform. At its best just east of Primrose, it rises to over 32 metres in height. It extends as far west as Shelburne, north to Horning's

Spring in Dufferin County. Airport Road near Highway 89, 1950.

Mills and south past Orangeville. In many places trees disguise its characteristic hummocky terrain, but it's clearly evident in both Mono and Mulmur.

The Orangeville Moraine plays an important role in keeping our water clean. Rain that has picked up contaminants from the air and on land eventually percolates through a moraine's sand and gravel. This action naturally cleanses this precious natural resource so that it returns to groundwater systems clean and potable. For this reason, protecting moraines from development is paramount to our continued good health.

Another moraine, the Singhampton Moraine, merges with yet a third, the Gibraltar, in rocky Dufferin County. The Singhampton Moraine is best seen between Honeywood and Black Bank, where it reaches a height of 25 metres in some places. The Orangeville and combined Singhampton and Gibraltar moraines come together between the Pine and Hockley valleys, forming a somewhat lower rise that is evident as you travel east on Highway 89. Once beyond Primrose you climb over the Orangeville Moraine, descend into a valley and climb up the combined Singhampton and Gibraltar Moraines in Violet Hill before arriving in Rosemont.

The Lookout Trail in Mono Cliffs Provincial Park.

Murphy's Pinnacle, Boyne Valley Provincial Park.

The valley between the Orangeville and the Singhampton-Gibraltar moraines is the Violet Hill Meltwater Discharge Channel. It carried glacial meltwater the length of Dufferin County some 13,000 years ago. The rocky, in fact, gravelly, evidence of its passage attracts aggregate companies. Marking a course along the Niagara Escarpment's eastern side from north of Lavender on the Mulmur-Nottawasaga border past Black Bank, the channel crossed the Pine River valley. From Kilgorie it passed through the present-day site of Violet Hill and ran east of Mono Centre before reaching Orangeville and eventually Lake Erie. Ice in the channel blocked the east-west flow of huge rivers in what are now the Pine and Hockley valleys. When the ice melted, rivers returned but never regained their original vigour. This explains why these valleys dwarf the Pine and Nottawasaga Rivers.

The best place to see many of Dufferin County's geological features is Mono Cliffs Provincial Park. In this 750-hectare wonder, you can view the Niagara

The Nottawasaga River cuts through the Niagara Escarpment on its way to Georgian Bay.

Luther Marsh.

Escarpment's 30-metre cliffs, the Orangeville Moraine, Violet Hill Meltwater Discharge Channel and McCarston's Lake, Mono's only natural lake. The park has two of Dufferin County's three outliers. Streams that cut away at the escarpment face isolated large islands of dolostone-capped rock by a process called stream piracy, creating stranded cliffs known as outliers. (Dufferin's other outlier is near Black Bank in Mulmur.)

You can also walk among mature hardwood forests dominated by sugar maples and Eastern hemlocks. The park's viewing platforms allow visitors to look back at the cliff face where the roots of wizened Eastern white cedars miraculously maintain a foothold in the hard dolomite stone. Only a few centimetres in diameter, some of these rugged trees are 1,000 or more years old. The extremely rare Hart's tongue fern, the clever walking fern and the nationally rare rugulose grape fern (*Botrychium rugulosum*) make Mono Cliffs Park a Filicales-lovers delight. Incredibly, the park supports 44 of the 96 species of ferns and fern allies that grow in Ontario.

Springs that bubble up near McCarston's Lake mark the headwaters of the south tributary of Sheldon Creek. It eventually flows into one of Dufferin's four major rivers: the north-flowing Nottawasaga. The Nottawasaga meanders from its headwaters in Amaranth Township and then picks up speed through the Hockley Valley on its 122-kilometre journey to Georgian Bay. Considered a misfit river because it is too small a waterway to have carved out such a huge ravine, the Nottawasaga is mighty by Dufferin's standards. Because it was created by a river other than the misfit Nottawasaga, the Hockley Valley is a re-entrant valley.

A tributary to the Nottawasaga, the once-powerful Pine is another misfit river flowing in a re-entrant valley. It's hard to imagine today that the Pine River roared in the early 1900s, turning turbines that produced electricity for Shelburne, Orangeville and Horning's Mills. A few short decades later, loss of tree cover had stemmed its flow to little more than a trickle. It was insufficient for power production and unsuitable for indigenous salmon. Now that the trees have returned, however, the Pine boasts a healthy fish population and ideal recreational opportunities.

The Grand River, the second of Dufferin's four major rivers, travels southwest to Lake Erie. With its source in the northwest corner of Melancthon, the Grand picks up water from Boyne Creek, Willow Brook and the Luther Marsh, via Black Creek, before leaving Dufferin on its 300-kilometre trip. Early Native inhabitants recognized the grandness of the Grand River. They called it the Tinaatoua, which means rapid river. Over the years it was named Riviere Rapide and then Grande Riviere before taking on the anglicized title Grand River. Not surprisingly, the Grand River flows through Grand Valley.

Dufferin's other major waterways are the south-flowing Credit and Humber Rivers. The Credit—so named because European traders often gave goods to the Mississauga Natives on credit in exchange for promised furs—rises up north of Orangeville and travels through the town on its 68-kilometre journey to Lake Ontario in Mississauga. Although Dufferin County is home to only a small part of the Credit, it has more impact on this river than on any other of its major waterways. As it courses through Orangeville it picks up runoff from roads and lawns and receives treated effluent from Orangeville's sewage-treatment plant. So far, the natural action of the river successfully removes these pollutants, but additional growth in this expanding town could surpass the Credit's ability to cleanse itself. Due care must be given this proud river.

Hockley Bridge, built in 1908.

The headwaters of the main Humber River can be traced to Mono. The Humber also empties into Lake Ontario. Though some 750 streams drain into the Humber River, only a few of them are found in Dufferin County. Instead, the river appears as a complex web of small veins that meander across the flat lands in Peel and York Regions. Designated a Canadian Heritage River, the Humber didn't become the Humber until Sir John Graves Simcoe, Upper Canada's first lieutenant-governor, named it after the Humber River in Yorkshire, England. Previously, it was

Orangeville's Islands Lake.

known as the Tau-a-hon-ate, the Toronto River and the St. John's River. The latter name recognized St. Jean Baptiste Rousseau, the first European settler known to walk its banks.

Dufferin County, dubbed the High County and Headwaters Country because so many rivers emanate from its elevated heights, has another aquatic feature of note: the Luther Marsh. In 2000, the marsh, which straddles the border between Dufferin and Wellington counties, became an Important Bird Area of national significance since it supports migratory birds and provides habitat for the least bittern, a threatened species.

Covering an amazing 5,600 hectares, the Luther Marsh is an oasis for wildlife lovers. Designated an Area of Natural and Scientific Interest (ANSI) by the Ontario Ministry of Natural Resources and a provincially significant Class One wetland, the Luther Marsh is not a natural feature. Rather, it was created to control flooding and augment flow in the Grand River. Its wildlife attributes are but a lucky result.

It took two years, between 1952 and 1954, to turn what had been a large swamp surrounded by a few farms into a 2,300-hectare lake and extensive wetland complex. It now boasts 24 rare plants including *Valeriana uliginosa*, a provincially rare species. It has three regionally rare butterflies, two provincially rare reptiles and one uncommon amphibian. It has an active heronry; ospreys nest there and it is one of the southernmost nesting sites for loons. Blueberries grow in the 500-hectare Wylde Lake bog, and the Luther Marsh tied for tenth place of 1,800 areas in the province when the Breeding Bird Atlas project recorded 134 species of nesting birds in the Luther Marsh.

Ladyslippers thrive on the Niagara Escarpment.

Grand Valley.

Luther Marsh.

Luther Lake.

Local residents claim to have sighted bobcats and black bears, and now the Luther Marsh is expected to provide habitat for even more waterfowl. Completed in 2001, the Monticello Project is a 230-acre satellite wetland designed to attract black and Adwall ducks. It was partially paid for by a group of American duck hunters who discovered that most of the waterfowl they hunted in Ohio came from the Luther Marsh.

Along with the Wylde Lake bog, the largest undisturbed bog in south-central and southwestern Ontario, the Luther Marsh has all three other wetland types. There is a remarkable 17-hectare fen, a great deal of marsh and no shortage of swamp. Very few wetlands have all four categories represented. And to top it all off, the Egerton Esker crosses the Luther Marsh, an anomaly in a wetland complex. The Grand River Conservation Authority, which manages the area, once mined gravel from this esker to build roads, but it discontinued the practice when, because of the Egerton Esker's presence, the Luther Marsh was designated a regionally significant Earth Sciences ANSI — just one more feather in the Luther Marsh's considerable cap.

No description of Dufferin County's natural landscape is complete without a peek into one of the 150 or more bluebird boxes tirelessly monitored by Shelly Anderson. The fourth generation of Andersons to farm in Mono, Shelly was born in 1909. Now retired, he spends his time from early April until mid-August travelling from farm fields to neighbours' backyards. With nothing more than an aluminium stepladder, a pair of pliers and some material left over from abandoned birds' nests in the back of his pickup truck, he follows a well-worn route. Shelly apologizes, "I don't have time to bird watch." Instead, he says, "I'm too busy with the bluebirds."

At each stop, Shelly, or one of his willing assistants, climbs up to one of a pair of bird boxes, pulls the pins that release a wall and monitors what's happening inside. The range of possibilities is part of the intrigue. If, as the door is raised, a feather flutters in the wind, you know it's pesky tree swallows and not bluebirds that have set up a home in the box. For tree swallows, notoriously poor housekeepers, are pleased to take advantage of Shelly's carpentry.

If, however, when you slowly swing the door upward, you see a nest of twigs sometimes six or seven inches high and clean as a whistle, you'll know that Shelly's beloved bluebirds have made this box their home. With care you can reach into the nest to feel what's inside. Your fingers may come across four or

A grey treefrog.

Scott's Falls, once known as Canning's Falls.

Shelly Anderson checking his bluebirds.

Eastern bluebirds now flock to Dufferin County.

five pale blue eggs, smooth and still warm, or you might encounter small fledglings whose stubby blue pinfeathers indicate they will soon be ready for banding and forever be part of a registry set up in Washington, D.C. But nothing is quite as exciting as coming in contact with inch-long, hours-old birds. When you announce to Shelly that you've detected real young 'uns he always asks the same question: "Are they pink?" And then you get to climb a step higher and peer into the nest to determine if they are indeed pink and, as it turns out, somewhat furry.

Bluebirds require special habitat to thrive. They like wide-open spaces and short-cut grass, an environment that is also attractive to more common tree swallows. But Shelly's tireless monitoring, his arduous practice of removing the grubs that may kill bluebirds, and his construction of bluebird boxes mean that as many as 600 fledglings may be banded in a single season. As a result, it's not uncommon in Dufferin County to glimpse that unmistakable flash of blue that makes the once endangered Eastern bluebird such an exciting sight.

CHAPTER TWO

Up in Orange Country

"To me, Dufferin County is an ideal place to live. It is close enough to large urban centres to provide
necessary jobs and resources, yet far enough away, rugged enough, cold and wet enough,
to naturally resist the onslaught of big cities, big business and big agriculture."
—*Frank Abel, member of the Christadelphian Church, Shelburne.*

Lewis Burwell wrote of Luther in 1831: "I regret having to say that it is impossible ever to effect a settlement here;
for the whole township appears to be one continual swamp.... I therefore beg leave to suggest
the propriety of ordering the survey stopped, as the township can never be settled."

Luther and Melancthon, the names chosen for two of Dufferin's townships, hint at the theological conviction of early settlers. As the tale goes, these swampy, insect-ridden townships almost defeated crews sent out to open them up for settlement. When authorities denied their request to abandon the foolhardy task of surveying what they considered uninhabitable land, the surveyors, good Irish Catholics both, named the townships after the meanest men they knew: Martin Luther, the Protestant Reformer, and Phillip Melanchthon, Luther's co-worker.

It's not surprising that Roman Catholics would avoid places named Luther and Melancthon, but this doesn't explain fully why Dufferin's Roman Catholic population has always been well below the provincial average. The real answer involves timing. There were easier places to settle, so early pioneers passed Dufferin by. As a result, when economic refugees from Northern Ireland immigrated to North America around 1830, land was still available in the high county. Irish Protestants congregated in Mono and Mulmur, discouraging Roman Catholics from moving in.

An 1851 church survey tells the story: Roman Catholics were poorly represented in the area. And not much had changed 90 years later. In 1941, Dufferin had the lowest proportion of Roman

Community of Christ Church, north of Redickville.

Violet Hill, Loyal Orange Lodge, circa 1910.

Members of the Ladies Orange Benevolent Association, circa 1930.

Catholics of any of Ontario's 50 counties and districts. By 1971, Dufferin was no longer at the bottom of the heap, but with only 10 percent Catholics, it lagged well behind the provincial average of 33 percent.

The Irish Protestants who settled in Dufferin often organized their Orange Lodge before erecting a church. The Loyal Orange Lodges in what became Stanton, Purple Hill, Mono Mills and Orangeville started up in the early 1830s, whereas most churches didn't appear until at least a decade later.

Orange Lodges were first organized in Ireland in the 1790s to defend the Protestant religion after King James II attempted to re-establish Roman Catholicism as supreme over Church and State in England. At the invitation of a group of political parties opposed to James II, Prince William of Orange landed in Britain in 1688 and took the throne from James II in a bloodless coup, dubbed the Glorious Revolution. Two years later, on July 12, 1690, William once again defeated James II, this time at the Battle of the Boyne in Ireland. Hence, Orange Parades take place on July 12 and Dufferin County has a Boyne River.

Despite their anti-Roman Catholic stance, Orange Lodges were a great help to new settlers. They were at the centre of social life in many of Dufferin's fledgling communities. The July 12 picnic and parade was a major annual event and, as recently as 1962, the *Orangeville Banner* reported that Orangeville's Orange Parade was more than three miles long. By tradition, a local equestrian garbed in period dress astride a white horse was at the head of the procession. With an orange sash across his chest, this "King William of Orange" led the festive, if somewhat vexatious, parade.

Orange Parade in Shelburne, circa 1920. Note the white horses.

Orangeville held its last Orange Parade in the 1960s, whereas members of the Royal Oak Lodge No. 256 of Grand Valley believe Shelburne had parades as recently as the 1980s. At the turn of the millennium, only two Orange Lodges — Grand Valley Lodge No. 256, which meets in Waldemar, and the lodge in Mansfield — remained active in Dufferin County, down from the 66 Lodges that once shaped life in the high hills. (Interestingly, Orangeville was not named after the Orange Order, as many presume. Instead, it recognizes its founder, Orange Lawrence, who, ironically, didn't belong to an Orange Lodge.)

Dufferin's Protestants reportedly hated all Roman Catholics except, as Adelaide Leitch points out in

Into the High County, "those they knew personally as neighbours." This sentiment likely accounts for Dufferin's aborted attempt to put down an imagined Fenian uprising.

In 1866, just before Confederation, Dufferin's Catholic-fearing Protestants became frenzied as rumours that some Fenians — Irish-Americans hostile to British rule — had crossed the border and were garnering support from Catholics in Adjala Township to invade Dufferin. Ken Weber captured the scenario in *In the Hills* magazine: "Seems one of the Allens had been over at Mansfield, where he met a fellow from Camilla whose sister was being courted by a volunteer in the Caledon Infantry Company. According to the sister, the volunteer understood from Colonel Durie in Toronto that once the Fenians got up into the hills here, they'd arranged with the Catholics in Adjala to rise up and join them. Not only that, they'd already picked out farms for themselves in Mono and Mulmur!"

So when a call to arms came one night, some 400 men turned up in Rosemont wielding muskets, pitchforks and tree limbs. They were ready to spill the blood of their Catholic neighbours in Adjala…or at least the blood of the Catholics they didn't know. Fortunately, the voice of reason, Doc Robinson, who administered medicine in Adjala, ruled that night. Sent ahead to suss out the danger, the good doctor returned and reported that all the Catholics he could find were fast asleep in their beds. The Fenians posed no threat to Mono or Mulmur—not that night and, as it turned out, not ever.

Despite the strength of Orangeism in Dufferin County, there were a few Roman Catholic enclaves. Mono Mills, formerly known as Market Hill and McLaughlin's Mill before that, was the first place in Dufferin to be settled. (Located on the border between Dufferin and Caledon, Mono Mills has been claimed by both municipalities from time to time. Currently, Mono Mills is officially part of Caledon.) Michael McLaughlin, a Roman Catholic, arrived there in 1819 or 1820. He built a gristmill and, as the town's early name implies, was at the centre of all that went on. People had to set aside their religious ideologies to get on in Mono Mills, a town that challenged Orangeville as the area's commercial centre until the railway passed it by.

The King brothers, who ran a boot and shoe factory in Shelburne in the mid-1800s, dealt with the Protestant-Catholic issue a different way. More interested in commerce than religion, they painted one side of their building green to attract the Catholics in Melancthon and the other side orange to appeal to the Orangemen throughout the remainder of Dufferin.

Laurel's Lambs

In 1925, the Presbyterian, Methodist and Congregationalist churches merged to become the United Church of Canada. While the Methodists and Congregationalists came into the union en masse, the Presbyterians voted church by church in what were sometimes acrimonious and divisive battles. As a result, we see both United and Presbyterian churches today, but there have been no Methodist churches since the union. (Congregational churches never made much of an appearance in Dufferin.) This helps explain why Methodism may seem foreign even though the Methodist Church was one of the strongest in pioneer days. The United churches in Relessey, Primrose, Laurel, Monticello and Whittington, for example, were

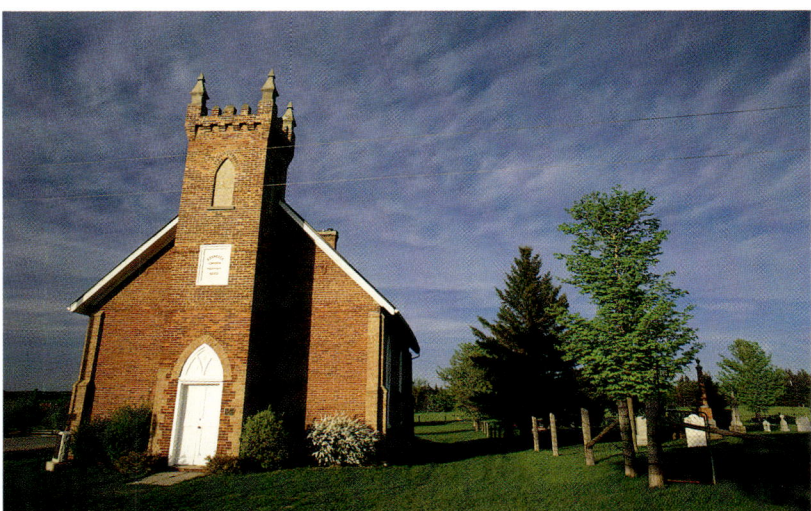

Ebenezer United Church, Relessey, built in 1870.

all Methodist at one time. (The Congregational Christian church that has occupied the old Baptist church on Zina Street in Orangeville since 1990 is not a Congregational church.)

Several things characterized the Methodists: they sang in church; served their congregations in the earliest days by sending out saddlebag preachers, also known as circuit riders; and during the mid-1800s they held spirited "camp" or revival meetings. For a week or more, generally between haying and harvesting, Methodists gathered in a forest to hear non-stop sermons given by a long lineup of preachers. So rowdy were these events that authorities questioned whether they were religious or social gatherings.

Despite their raucous camp meetings, Methodists were generally against alcohol consumption. Wine was banned from the Methodist Church in 1854 and is still uncommon in United churches.

Dufferin had its share of straight-laced Methodist communities, but Laurel, in Amaranth Township, was arguably the most prohibitionary of all. Called Richardson's Corners until the postmaster decided the name was too long and changed it to recognize his mother's fondness for the laurel bushes back in Ireland, Laurel was dry in the 1870s.

So when a group of men from Laurel, headed up by the Methodist minister, heard the Mansion House tavern in Shelburne was a bit slow to comply with the Canada Temperance, or Scott Act, that prohibited alcohol, they decided to take the law into their own hands. The men raided the hotel, forcing one patron to flee via an open window. They arrested the hotel-keeper, planning to take him to jail in Orangeville. But the people of Shelburne resented the Laurel invasion. They pelted the prohibitionists with snowballs and firecrackers and cheered when the editor of Orangeville's *Dufferin Post* dubbed them the Laurel Lambs.

A FOWL SUPPER

It wasn't only the Methodists who had rigid rules. The early Presbyterians were a rather dour group with a convention or two of their own. Organs were not allowed in most Presbyterian churches before 1875, though the church permitted singing of Psalms and a few scriptures. And unlike most denominations, the Presbyterians once stood to pray and sat to sing.

Alexander Lewis was Dufferin's first resident Presbyterian minister. Buried in Mono (though it's spelled "Mona" on his grave marker), Lewis led congregations throughout the area during the late 1830s and early 1840s. He built Mono's first Presbyterian church north of Mono Mills in 1838 and

Corbetton Methodist Parsonage.

Mulmur Methodist Cemetery, 5th Line.

was part of the opening ceremonies when a stone church, now long gone, opened in 1867. The enterprising Lewis was also the postmaster in Mono Mills, a magistrate and a Crown Land agent.

A little farther north, in Mansfield, lived a group of strong Presbyterians also served by Alexander Lewis. They travelled to a log church in Rosemont until they had their own. In preparation for their first resident minister, villagers built a manse in a field in 1853. It is believed to be the source of the town's name. Having voted down the union in 1925, St. Andrew's in Mansfield is an active Presbyterian church.

One of the events that keeps the St. Andrew's congregation together is its annual Fowl Supper. As is so often the case, this fund-raising, community-galvanizing event was the brainchild of the churchwomen. The first recorded Fowl Supper in St. Andrew's church basement was in 1892, though it began before that in the hamlet of Stanton.

These days, about 450 people from near and far fill up on turkey and goose, potatoes, peas, carrots, preserves and scrumptious pies. The Fowl Supper, explains Shirley Orr, who has been attending the supper since before she was born, is so noisy "you

St. Francis of Assisi Cemetery, Mono Mills.

couldn't hear a cannon drop." When the event outgrew the church basement it moved to the Orange Hall. This venue has caused some confusion for out-of-towners. Norma Gallaugher recalls telling a lady from Mississauga to come to the Orange Hall. Unable to find an orange-coloured building, the woman almost missed supper.

Proving that old ways die hard, St. Andrew's Fowl Supper is held on the first Saturday in November, to be close to Guy Fawkes Day. This English celebration recognizes the Gunpowder Plot. On November 5, 1605, a group of Catholics led by Fawkes attempted to blow up the House of Lords in England to protest the severity of penal laws against the practice of Catholicism. Their plot mysteriously given away, the conspirators were imprisoned or executed. To this day, the English celebrate November 5 with fireworks and bonfires on which they burn effigies of the conspirators. In Canada, November 5 is celebrated by Fowl or Oyster Suppers.

AN IRASCIBLE OLD MAN

That Dufferin County celebrates Guy Fawkes Day shouldn't be a surprise, since many settlers were members of the Church of England. And like this explosive celebration, the Church of England arrived in Dufferin with a bang. When he was almost 60 years old, a very colourful Seneca Ketchum took up land in the community of Purple Hill, next door to today's Orangeville. Though never ordained by the Church of England, he came to preach and was licensed as the "Missionary of the Township of Mono" in 1830 by Bishop John Strachan himself. He built one of the area's earliest churches in 1837. It was a log building known as St. Mark's Anglican Church.

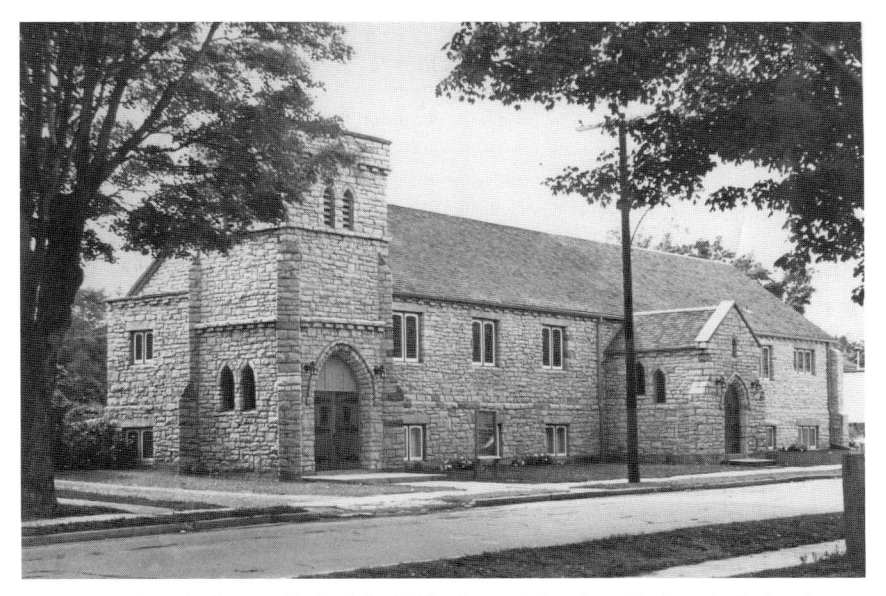

Tweedsmuir Church, Orangeville, built in 1940, of stone taken from the Canada Portland Cement factory.

Remembered as an irascible old man, Ketchum had a fervent missionary zeal that pitted him against a rival Church of England. Championed by Squire George McManus, Old St. John's Anglican Church on Mono's 7th Line served a bustling community. So both Squire McManus and Ketchum vied to have Reverend John Fletcher, a young Irishman sent out in 1848 to become the "Traveling Missionary for the Simcoe District," resident in their church.

Ketchum virtually kidnapped Fletcher's family after they innocently accepted an invitation to stay at his home until the rectory was completed. But Reverend Fletcher couldn't be won over, so Ketchum, who was referred to as "earnest-minded but not very sane" by an archdeacon of the church, travelled to Toronto to insist of Bishop Strachan that Reverend Fletcher be

Old St. John's Anglican Church, 7th Line, Mono, built in 1878.

permanently assigned to his part of the parish. Any hope of that eventuality was dashed that day. Appalled by the audaciousness of Ketchum's request, Bishop Strachan instructed Reverend Fletcher: "You are not to give way to any of his [Ketchum's] improprieties, and if he acts at all, he must only act in obedience to your directions...."

Though he remained in the area for 20 years, Ketchum died before the church separated his parish from Mono Mills. But this didn't stop the childless Ketchum from leaving his considerable land holdings —over 600 acres—to his beloved church. His famous brother, Jesse, however, contested this generous action. A member of the Upper Canada Legislature, the younger Ketchum managed to keep his brother's land so he could turn it over to his son, Jesse Ketchum III.

Seneca Ketchum's legacy lives on. St. Mark's brick church in Orangeville sits on land once owned by this pious churchman. A church plaque recognizes Seneca Ketchum for dedicating his life to the parish and Jesse Ketchum III for donating the land on which the church stands.

A Spiritual Evolution

Protestants still dominate Dufferin's population in the new millennium, but that hasn't stopped other churches from opening their doors and changing forever the county's social fabric. Dutch immigrants who arrived in Canada after the Second World War brought their own churches. The Canadian Reformed (in Orangeville and Grand Valley) and Christian Reformed (on Blind Line) churches are both Dutch Reformed Churches. They attract almost 1,000 members, many of whom are not Dutch descendants.

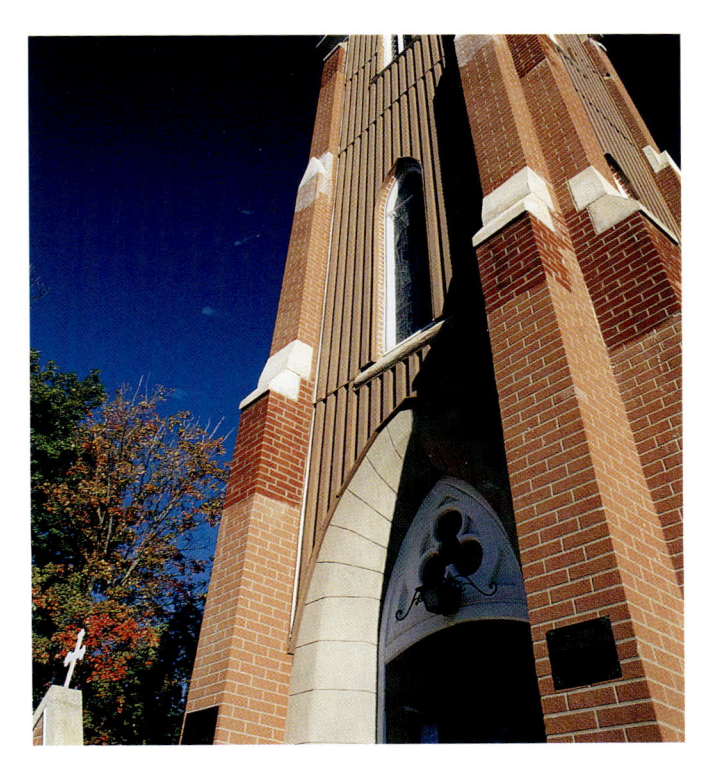

St. Mark's Anglican Church, Orangeville.

The Holy Mother of God Monastery on Mono's 7th Line might be best known for the perogies, beeswax candles and honey it sells, but some 90 people attend this Ukrainian Catholic Church. They hear the Divine Liturgy of St. John Chrysostom and can enjoy the lovely grounds that surround this establishment. There is a Baptist church on the Hockley Road near Highway 10 and several congregations of Jehovah's Witnesses. About 60 Christadelphians, who take the Bible at its word, meet every Sunday in Amaranth. Their fundamental religion heralds from the American Civil War. On Airport Road just north of Mono Mills a large sign announces the International Taoist Tai Chi Centre of Canada. Master Moy Lin-shin developed the special form of Tai Chi offered at the 40-hectare centre. It cultivates health and vitality of body and spirit. Master Moy studied in China and Hong Kong for over 30 years before bringing his unique brand of Tai Chi to North America. Regular classes and workshops are held throughout the year at this tremendous facility.

There's a popular candlelight service on Christmas Eve at the beautifully restored Whitfield Anglican Church. Over 100 people attend to hear the Eucharist before lighting a candle and singing "Silent Night" in the eerie darkness. The Primrose United Church hosts a Pork Barbecue each May and the Camilla United Church puts on a Strawberry Supper in June. Still without electricity, the Relessey United Church stokes up its pot-bellied stove for an old-fashioned carol service on a Sunday in mid-December, and Shelburne's Trinity United Church now has two Christmas Eve services to meet the demand. The non-denominational, completely restored Mitchell Church (also the Yellow Briar Church, for those familiar with the book *The Yellow Briar*) is a popular spot for weddings. It holds an anniversary service each June.

Still largely the domain of Protestants, Dufferin's religious mix is much richer these days. Though some churches may be struggling with dwindling congregations, the crowds flocking to the Canadian Reformed Church and the Taoist Tai Chi Centre point to an evolving rather than a diminishing state of spirituality in Dufferin County.

Camilla United Church Women's group, Camilla.

Shrigley Church, Melancthon.

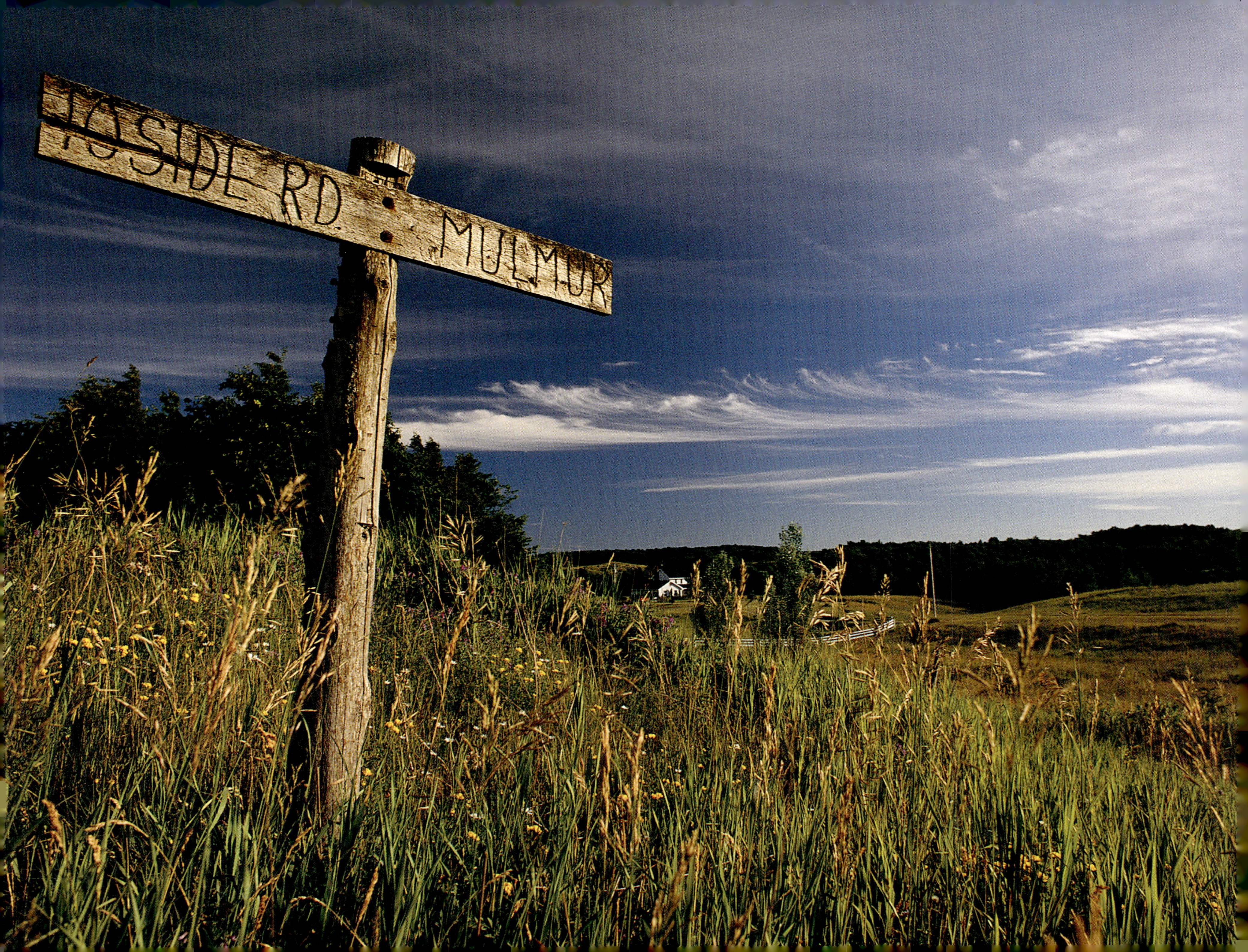
10 SIDE RD
MULMUR

CHAPTER THREE

Rails, Trails, But No Highwaymen

"I love the fact that I can stand on a hill just a few blocks from my home, turn in any direction and love what I see."
—*JoAnn Pilkey, Orangeville resident*

"It still feels pretty comfortable to me. All my friends I grew up with are from there."
—*Gordon Townsend, age 74. The farm he grew up on lies beneath the Luther Marsh.*

In 1830, when Lewis Horning trekked from Hamilton to what would become Horning's Mills, the last leg of his trip was not for the faint of heart. Their wagons overflowing with supplies, Lewis and his entourage of carpenters, millers and blacksmiths hacked and chopped their way for the final 26 miles through unbroken forest and across swamps and rivers.

In York (now Toronto), authorities knew that few immigrants had Horning's determination. They needed roads if they were to settle in Upper Canada. So the government of the day ordered surveyors to lay out colonization roads and set about having them constructed. But Orangeville seemed to be as high as the road builders cared—or were ordered—to go. Settlers who came to what would be Dufferin County had to follow trails made by the Native people or by men such as Lewis Horning.

In keeping with the lack of interest in colonizing Dufferin's high hills, Hurontario Street, its first main road, was a not a colonization road at all. Instead, it was a communication road meant to link Toronto to Collingwood. Dufferin just happened to lie in between. When Sir John Graves Simcoe moved the capital of Upper Canada from Newark to York he exchanged fear of invasion from the United States for possible attacks by Natives. His solution was to link York with his

At the crossroads, west of Mansfield.

Orangeville, Prince of Wales Road, looking south from near Third Street.

military installations. This resulted in plans for Yonge Street to join Toronto and Barrie, Dundas Street to provide a link to the west and Hurontario Street to hook up Port Credit and Collingwood.

Fairly well constructed to the south and the north of Dufferin by the 1830s, Hurontario Street was still nothing more than a blazed trail through Mono and Mulmur. It wasn't until 1850 that it was finished all the way to Nottawasaga Bay, and it wasn't the government that finally filled in the gap. With a desperate need to get to markets in Brampton and Collingwood, settlers turned the muddy trail into a road that, at least during the winter when it was frozen, could be navigated by oxen or horse and sleigh.

Today, Hurontario Street can cause some confusion. In Caledon, Highway 10 and Hurontario Street are one and the same. Between Highway 9 and Highway 89, however, Highway 10 abandons the route surveyed back in the early 1800s. It shifts one line west and follows the flatter Prince of Wales Road (named in honour of Queen Victoria's son, Prince Edward, after he visited Canada in 1860).

But Hurontario Street still exists as a seldom-travelled gravel road through Mono. And Mulmur's Centre Road, a lovely twisting route that plunges down into the Pine River valley, is also a remnant of Hurontario Street. One indication of the former importance of these roads is the use of WHS and EHS on area road signs. They tell you whether you are east or west of Hurontario Street.

Ken Gamble, born in 1930, recalls that Highway 10 was no cakewalk when he was growing up in Shelburne. Elba Hill just south of Highway 89 is identifiable today because if its communication tower. Back then it used to be far steeper and there were no passing lanes. During all-too-frequent winter storms it was impossible to navigate and then, in spring, the highway flooded in the swampy section to the south.

At Highway 89, Highway 10 turns west and then northwest as it makes its way to Owen Sound. Called the Toronto-Sydenham Road because it linked Toronto and Sydenham (now Owen Sound), it has also been known as the Toronto Line, Rankin Road, the Gravel Road and, more recently, Highway 10. It also formed the baseline for the Toronto Sydenham Survey.

Surveyor Charles Rankin received orders in 1848 to "Commence your operations by drawing a direct line from the north-west angle of the 4th concession of the township of Amaranth to the rear of the 3rd concession of the township of Holland, which is intended to form part of a leading road from the city of Toronto to Sydenham on Owen Sound, Lake Huron…." Rankin was to also survey lots of 50 acres alongside the new road (though they ranged from 23 acres to 90 acres because of the meanderings of the road) and number them starting with Lot 1 in Holland and ending with Lot 300 in Melancthon. The resulting survey through Melancthon, referred to as the Toronto Sydenham Survey, turned out to be one of only a few instances in Ontario where concession roads do not parallel any of the township borders.

Settlers were generally offered 50-acre lots for free with the opportunity to double their holding if they met certain requirements such as clearing a specified portion of the land, building a house and planting crops.

And until the 1920s, landowners also had to perform labour under the Statute Labour Act. Land grants required settlers to spend a certain number of days building and maintaining concession roads and sideroads. If they failed to fulfil this duty, a penalty was levied against their taxes.

Through this system of indentured labour, Dufferin ended up with its grid pattern of roads, some of which have intriguing names. Back Line (Second Line SW) in Melancthon, for example, was so named because it was behind the first range of lots laid out west of the Toronto-Sydenham Road. Two stories account for Mono's Blind Line. One says that because it ends abruptly near Orangeville and, before there was a bridge, stopped short of the Nottawasaga River, it was

Airport Road.

Con Smythe's truck in deep snow on Highway 9.

House of Jelly, Shelburne.

"blind." The other claims that seven blind pigs once lived on the road. This version is all the more intriguing, since "blind pig" is slang for a speakeasy or bar that sells liquor illegally. Dumby's Road in Mono may have been named after a farmer who lived on it. Friends nicknamed him Doc Dombey (sounds like Dumby) after a Charles Dickens character.

DUFFERIN AND ITS IRON HORSE

Though the train arrived in Orangeville in 1871, it didn't reach Shelburne for another two years. It was amid frenzied excitement that several small coaches and a baggage car powered by a locomotive named *Owen Sound* rounded a corner and pulled into Shelburne on a splendid spring day in 1873. Having left Toronto at 8 A.M., and after several stops along the way, it appeared just past noon. Buried under an army of enthusiastic passengers who clung to any handhold, the train had to stop short of the newly built station to avoid running over the cheering crowd. It seemed the entire town turned out to welcome the coal-powered iron horse. Following a short reception, Shelburne's founding father, William Jelly, invited the entire entourage to dinner. The ensuing party may have gone on all night had the steam train not been scheduled to arrive in Owen Sound at 8 P.M.

Before the Toronto, Grey & Bruce arrived in Shelburne, a stage line was the only form of public transit and it was a slow trip along rough roads. So the TG&B was instantly popular with passengers and for freight, but there were problems too. After much consideration, the TG&B's owners had elected to build a narrow-gauge line. Rather than the standard 4 feet, 8 inches between rails, the TG&B was only 3 feet, 6 inches wide. Reducing construction costs drove the decision and it did lower expenses—though not as much as anticipated—but the narrow-gauge train carried less freight, and when it reached Toronto its cargo had to be transferred to standard-gauge trains. Any construction savings were quickly erased.

When the Credit Valley Railway between Streetsville and Orangeville opened in 1879, the added competition convinced the TG&B's owners to upgrade the line to the wider gauge. In 1881, all the rails were pulled up, the engines and railcars replaced, and many of the curves and bridges along the line widened to accommodate larger trains. The wider gauge also helped solve another serious problem that had plagued the small narrow locomotives.

The TG&B travelled through one of Ontario's snowiest regions. Old timers who remember Dufferin's fierce winter storms won't be surprised to learn that snow frequently defeated the small wood-burning engines. At an infamously snowy spot between Shelburne and Melancthon, during a particularly wintry 1874, 18-foot drifts overwhelmed a plough-less locomotive. When every effort to release the train failed, there was no choice but to leave it put until warm spring weather could accomplish what shovels had failed to do.

Down in Amaranth things weren't much better. After the train became snowbound one too many

Orangeville Junction at Fraxa, where the Teeswatch Branch left the TG&B mainline.

Dufferin has a unique and varied terrain.

times near Laurel, the TG&B loaded the Laurel station onto a train car and took it away. It was only returned after Amaranth Township provided a new, less snowy location and agreed to clear the access road.

By 1905, the TG&B had bigger engines but that didn't mean all snow-related concerns were solved. That year, six locomotives and a plough made their way through blinding snow from Crombie's Station (the building that housed this small flag stop is preserved in the Dufferin County Museum) to Shelburne. Unwisely, three of the engines and the plough returned immediately to Crombie's Station for water. When they failed to reappear, the three engines still in Shelburne headed south to find out what had happened. The trains met head on. Thankfully only one man was killed in what was one of a multitude of train wrecks in Dufferin County. And snow wasn't the only culprit. In 1879, the *Sun* newspaper in Orangeville complained that train derailments were a daily occurrence because of the poor condition of the TG&B's tracks.

Neither snow nor poor tracks caused the most famous crash along the line. Though it didn't happen within Dufferin County's borders, it involved a train carrying passengers from Orangeville and points north to attend the Canadian National Exhibition in Toronto. The Horseshoe Curve in Caledon, as the name implies, was very tight. It allowed trains to negotiate the 120-metre Niagara Escarpment. At one point, trains descended 26 metres in less than a half a kilometre. On September 3, 1907, the engineer was likely travelling a bit too fast as he made his way down the mountain. The train derailed, killing 7 people and injuring 113 more.

Another steep route was the section between Orangeville and Fraxa Junction (called Orangeville

Railway ties, Orangeville. Prince of Wales Road, also known as First Street.

Rotary steam snow shovel, invented in Dufferin County.

Horseshoe train wreck, September 3, 1907: 7 killed, 113 injured.

Junction until 1908). Steve Brown, the archivist at the Dufferin County Museum, recalls seeing the helper engines that pushed trains up the incline deadhead back to Orangeville once their work was done.

Once the train arrived in Fraxa Junction it could continue north on the mainline or head west on the Teeswater Branch. This line of the TG&B, completed in 1873, travelled west to Teeswater via Grand Valley. Plans to extend the Teeswater line to Wingham and Kincardine never materialized, but the branch was a boon to the communities along its route.

The small town of Waldemar, for a time, was the biggest winner of all along the line. When East Luther Township protested the train's late arrival by withholding the $500 it was supposed to pay to the TG&B, the railway retaliated by not building a station in Grand Valley. As a result, all freight and passengers ended up in Waldemar. It took East Luther and the

The Orangeville-Brampton Railway, formerly the TG&B.

Mono Cliffs Inn, Mono Centre.

TG&B about five years to work out their differences. When they did, Grand Valley got its station and Waldemar began its slow decline. But for a time, Waldemar bustled with activity.

Throughout Southern Ontario, towns that were little more than flag stops or that failed to get the railway at all waned as their neighbours with stations prospered. Likely the most dramatic example in Dufferin County involved Orangeville and Mono Mills. Though these towns are hardly comparable today, until the arrival of the train they were close competitors.

As the story goes, Mono Mills got a little too greedy as rumours of the train began to circulate. When TG&B officials arrived in town, residents demanded too much for their land and the TG&B selected a different, less costly route through Orangeville. Furthermore, Mono Mills was a very rough place. As the TG&B officials made their way about town they reportedly witnessed some twelve fistfights in progress at one time, a factor that presumably influenced their decision.

And the train's arrival had another side effect that landowners failed to be compensated for. Old timers recall that the work crews who built the lines wiped out local rabbits and groundhogs by snaring them to supplement their diets.

Orangeville, for a few years, had two train lines, two stations and a spur line that connected the TG&B's station to quarries in the Hockley Valley. The northern terminus of the Credit Valley Railway that shuttled between Orangeville and Streetsville was at Fourth Street, on the north side of Broadway. The station, consisting of coaling sheds, a water tower, freight sheds, a turntable, repair facilities and sidings, closed in 1884.

Railway turntable, Orangeville, south of the Townline, 1900.

The TG&B made its stop south of the Townline. It offered incoming passengers a number of services, especially after 1909, when it added an excellent restaurant. When the train arrived, the restaurant's proprietor would ring a large brass bell to entice visitors to patronize his establishment.

The TG&B also had the better stationhouse. In *Meet Me at the Station*, author Elizabeth Willmot describes the Orangeville station: "Occasionally a house or public building acquires an indefinable romantic quality. When you see the CPR [TG&B] station in Orangeville you are aware of that unexplainable phenomenon...." Built sometime between 1905 and 1907, it replaced a more basic station and had a lovely circular waiting room. As passenger service on the line declined and then ended altogether, an elaborate station was no longer required. It was sold in the 1980s, and the new owners moved the entire edifice to its current site on Armstrong Street in 1988.

After a slow trip east on the Townline and west on Broadway, the over-sized load had to fit between the buildings that separated Broadway from the station's new home. The only damage occurred when the station rubbed up against a dinosaur painted on the narrow alleyway wall and, still in evidence today, scraped a bit of colour from the critter's neck.

Once landed, the station's round waiting room became a small café, and the back portion was converted into an antique shop. In 1995, new owners completely renovated the building and a year later it became a lovely restaurant, fittingly named the Old Train Station.

During the steam era, eight passenger trains a day stopped in Orangeville. The elegant Steamship Express passed by daily on its way to Owen Sound, where passengers boarded a ship and sailed to Sault Ste. Marie and could then travel to the western frontier.

The TG&B train station became a restaurant after it was moved to its Armstrong Street location in 1988.

The Globe, Rosemont.

Mixed trains that carried passengers and freight travelled through Orangeville and on to Fraxa Junction, where they could turn west and followed the Teeswater Branch. But the convenience of motorcars spelled death to the trains, and the epoch of travel by rail came crashing down in the early to mid-1900s.

The romantic era of the railways was especially short-lived in Dufferin. In 1883, Ontario & Quebec Railway (O&Q) leased both the TG&B and the Credit Valley Railway. Soon they were part of the O&Q's parent company, the Canadian Pacific Railway. Trains got smaller and ran less frequently. Diesel engines replaced steam locomotives. Stations that once bustled with passengers and overflowed with freight were reduced to mere flag stations before the CPR closed and demolished them altogether.

The last passenger train ran through Orangeville in 1970. But for a time, it appeared as if a tourist train might ply the seldom-used tracks. In 1973, a resplendent reconditioned steam locomotive, pulling refurbished

A well-known landmark—the Superburger in Primrose.

coaches named after stops along the Credit Valley Railway (CVR), made a grand show. For a short time it carried tourists from Toronto along the CVR route to Orangeville, where it picked up the TG&B line to Owen Sound. But negotiations to continue this service failed, and before long the engine and coaches were moved and became part of the South Simcoe Railway.

Then, in the 1990s, CP Rail pulled up all the rails along both the TG&B's main line and the Teeswater Branch.

But the rumble of the train wasn't entirely lost, at least in Orangeville. While the TG&B line sat silent and abandoned, CP Rail continued to run a small freight service on the old Credit Valley Railway line between Streetsville and Orangeville. A few short years later, however, even Orangeville's freight train was threatened. In 1994, CP Rail announced plans to close the line and put it up for sale. With great vision, Orangeville saved the day. Recognizing how important rail transportation was to its manufacturing community and after a good deal of often tense negotiations, the Town of Orangeville patched together the $3.5 million it needed to close the deal and keep the train running. Nowadays, the Orangeville-Brampton Railway schedules two return trains per week between Brampton and Orangeville. Their sole function is to deliver supplies to manufacturers situated along the route. For the first time in years, improvements are being made to the line and plans are afoot to bring in a tourist train. It would transport passengers from Mississauga or Toronto over the trestle in the picturesque Forks of the Credit, climb up the Niagara Escarpment and bring them into Orangeville to shop or attend the theatre.

And there is more good news on the railway front. Negotiations are underway to determine if the Orangeville-Brampton Railway can acquire the old TG&B right-of-way between Orangeville and Amaranth. Rails and ties would have to be re-laid, but a train along this long-abandoned line would tie in one of Dufferin's major agricultural suppliers and presumably attract other businesses to set up shop along the route. It would also reverse the trend whereby railway tracks are being torn up, and mark Dufferin as a true promoter of what must surely become a more common means of sustainable transportation.

The Rosemont General Store.

Fairbairn Mileage Station, on Broadway in Orangeville, destroyed by fire in 2002.

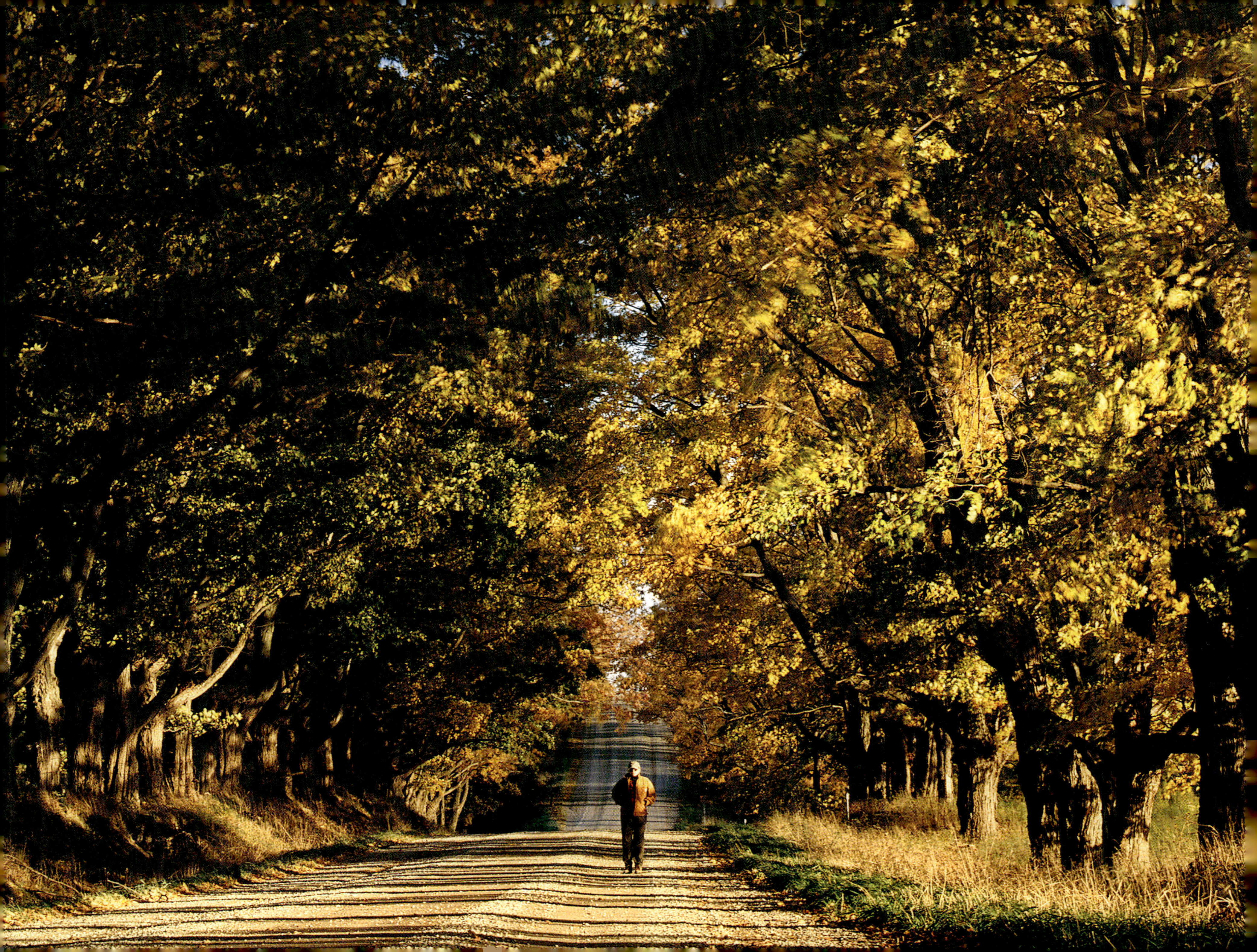

CHAPTER FOUR

Dufferin's Laborious Birth

"What originally brought us here, simply put, would be the small-town atmosphere, the fresh air and quiet nights, the dark skies made for stargazing, the beauty of the landscape where five minutes travel finds you beyond town limits and in the warm embrace of nature. What's kept us here for years is all of that and more: discovering a flourishing, creative community that is both inspired and inspirational makes this 'home' in every sense of the word."
—*Laura Bird, 43, and Javier Santamaria, 42, founding members of the Headwaters Acoustic Music Society, Orangeville.*

"My relatives have lived in every municipality in Dufferin County except the Township of East Garafraxa and before Dufferin County existed in the Counties of Simcoe and Grey. Thus, it wasn't easy for me to leave Dufferin County…."
—*William Church, Q.C., B.A., LL.B., born in Orangeville in 1933.*

To understand modern-day Dufferin County, look to its past. Dufferin experienced a laborious birth scarred by intrigue and politics. Its creation involved a power struggle between those who stood to benefit and those convinced that little good would come from Dufferin's unlikely amalgamation. It was a 17-year-long battle that ebbed and flowed as forces both within and outside Dufferin's borders challenged the convictions of its supporters.

The bickering and jealousies that characterized Dufferin's gestational period didn't diminish after the vote in 1879 that paved the way for Dufferin's birth in 1881. But they help account for the strength with which residents identify with their respective townships. Those long-ago events set a rocky foundation that teeters even today as history continues to repeat itself in what remains Southern Ontario's smallest and youngest county.

It all began in 1862 at the corner of Broadway and Mill Street in George Bell's Orangeville hotel. On an otherwise uneventful July night, twelve of Orangeville's most prominent businessmen and leaders gathered over drinks to discuss their community's future. Before leaving Bell's Hotel, one of Orangeville's

It's hard to imagine "The Maples" was once a bustling community.

Broadway, Orangeville, circa 1890, looking east from First Street.

few licensed establishments, Jesse Ketchum III, Thomas Jull, William Armstrong, William Parsons, Thomas Jackson, James Kelly, S. H. McKitrick, D. Youmans, J. Carbert, Falkner C. Stewart, T. R. Buckman and Dr. W. S. Hewat had passed a resolution that would eventually result in the vote that created Dufferin County. It would also ensure their town received the political and economic perks that came with the county town status.

In their conservative black coats, sombre beards and squarely perched hats, these gentlemen audaciously resolved: "That it is highly desirable that a new county to consist of the townships of Mono, Mulmur, Amaranth, Melancthon, Caledon and the east halves of Luther and Proton (to compose one township) and the east half of Garafraxa to be formed into a new County, said County to be called 'Hurontario County.'"

It's no wonder the resolution ruffled feathers. At the time, Melancthon and Shelburne were part of Grey County; Luther, East Garafraxa, Amaranth and Orangeville hailed from Wellington; and both Mono and Mulmur were in Simcoe. Slow to attract pioneers and several days away from their seats of government in Barrie, Sydenham (Owen Sound) and Guelph, these sparsely populated townships shared a feeling of isolation. But more than an occasional wish for local self-government was needed to bind together this otherwise ragtag collection of independent municipalities.

Even the landscape lacked uniformity. The flat lands of Melancthon and Amaranth were rough on early settlers. Late springs and early autumn frosts in these townships tested the mostly Irish settlers accustomed to their homeland's more temperate climate. Mulmur, with its deep valleys and soaring vistas, seemed close to the top of the world. The mighty Niagara Escarpment defined much of Mono's rocky landscape. Mono or Mona, as old timers call it, had an extra few frost-free days that made all the difference at harvest time. Garafraxa, the source of its name more likely a play on Spanish words than a reference to the small sassafras tree, mixed swampland with gravel deposits, whereas Luther's boggy landscape defeated more than one valiant land surveyor.

In 1863, a year after those twelve gentlemen made known their wishes for a new county, Orangeville was incorporated, a necessary move if Orangeville was to be named the county town. At the time, William Jelly had not yet ventured west from Leeds County to found what would later become Shelburne. Nonetheless, Shelburne would grow to resent Orangeville's success.

In 1874, the Ontario Legislature passed the Act that allowed a provisional council to be set up and the vote for a new county to be taken. The council would represent five townships: Amaranth, Mono, Mulmur, Melancthon and East Garafraxa. Luther was excluded. It also specified that Orangeville would be the county town and that the decision to become a new county would be determined in an open vote as opposed to a secret ballot.

Though Shelburne was never in the running for Dufferin's capital, merchants and village leaders believed their centrally located community should be awarded all the trappings associated with this political designation: the courthouse, jail, registry office and prestige. This was particularly true when Shelburne began the process of incorporation and finally achieved its goal in 1879.

Dufferin's gestational period stretched on as support for the new county mirrored the region's economic well-being. During periods of prosperity, supporters of

Looking east on Main Street, Shelburne, winter 1902.

Boyne Mill.

the union would push for a vote. When times were tough, those in favour backed off. They wondered if a fledgling new county would have the economic might to survive on its own. Bickering between townships and among towns and villages continued, further strengthening residents' ties to their local communities.

The editor of the *Sun* ranted in 1879: "Will the County of Dufferin be ever separated from the Counties of Wellington, Grey and Simcoe?" Then finally, on July 15, 1879, the Provisional Council met. Falkner Stewart, one of the participants in that meeting at George Bell's hotel in 1862, presided. A respected community leader, he operated a general store on Broadway for almost 40 years. He became Dufferin County's first warden and was eventually elected to Ontario's Legislature. Orangeville's Faulkner Street (despite the incorrect spelling) and Stewart Court were both named after this historic figure.

Decision to Form Dufferin County
Results from August 12, 1879

Municipality	For	Against
Melancthon	57	435
Mulmur	1	635
Amaranth	408	148
Mono	484	194
East Garafraxa	449	16
Orangeville	572	2
Total	1971	1430
Shelburne*	39	122
Rosemont*	20	118

(*The votes from Shelburne and Rosemont were included in the township votes.)

A month later, on August 12, 1879, the open vote took place. The northern townships flatly rejected the union. In Mulmur, the result was one for and 635 against. Melancthon followed a similar pattern, and Shelburne also turned it down. But the more densely populated southern municipalities had their way. In the end, the majority carried the day as 1,971 cried "yea" and only 1,430 called out "nay" in the open ballot.

Still another eighteen months would pass after the ballots had been cast before Dufferin County could be formed. In the interim, the provisional county fulfilled the terms of its incorporation by building the courthouse, jail and registry office in Orangeville. All located on Zina Street—named after Charlesina Hope Manners McCarthy, whose son Maitland, Dufferin's first county judge, donated the land where the courthouse and jail were built—they are fine examples of Ontario architecture.

Recognizing Canada's third governor general, Frederick Temple Blackwood, 1st Marquess of Dufferin and Ava, Dufferin County was officially proclaimed on Saturday, January 22, 1881. It came into effect two

Rock Hill Park, Mulmur.

days later. Shortly thereafter, on January 25, the first county council met with Falkner Stewart, Dufferin's first warden, presiding. The *Sun* announced: "Dufferin! Hatched at Last!"

Hatched, yes, but one happy family, not quite. Though the animosity between townships, towns and villages has mellowed over the years, Dufferin remains a collection of independent municipalities.

An attempt in 1999 to eliminate lower-tier (township) councils and adopt a regional form of government similar to its neighbour, Peel Region, demonstrated that urban and rural interests remain unaligned in Dufferin County.

County buildings, Orangeville.

At the urging of the provincial government, Orangeville and Shelburne joined forces that year to push through a proposal that very nearly came into effect. It would have created wards to replace townships and towns. The new, borderless "City of Dufferin" was to have thirteen ward councillors and a mayor. Each ward was to have one councillor except Mono, which would have had two, and Orangeville, which would have had five.

Orangeville, according to then deputy mayor Steve White, was "bedevilled by boundaries." A single-tier setup would remove borders, giving Orangeville access to the rivers and surrounding farmland it needed for expansion. With support from Orangeville, Shelburne and East Garafraxa, County Council had enough votes to approve the City of Dufferin option. In doing so, the plan was also passed by councils representing the majority of citizens. However, with only three of Dufferin's eight councils on side, the option did not meet the provincially legislated "triple majority" (support by county council, support by the majority of residents and support by the majority of lower-tier councils). As a result, and by the narrowest of margins, it did not come into effect.

Undeterred, supporters of the proposal asked the provincial government to send in a commissioner to resolve the impasse. Since the province favoured single-tier solutions, a commissioner was expected to impose this option. But the minister of Municipal Affairs at the time refused Dufferin's request, responding that he was "not satisfied that all local efforts to reach an agreement have been exhausted." At this juncture, it's fair to say that governance in Dufferin had come to a standstill. No decisions could be made at County Council since politicians on each side of the debate

Mulmur—the view from on high.

had dug in so deeply they were unable to speak to one another, much less reach an agreement. It's unclear where the impasse might have ended up if factors beyond Dufferin's borders hadn't saved the day.

Restructuring was a pet project of the provincial government. As more and more communities across the province followed the directive from Queen's Park, however, it became obvious that reducing the size and complexity of municipal governments was not resulting in the cost savings or the political brownie points that had been expected. The Ontario premier backed down from his demands and the pressure on Dufferin to amalgamate came off at almost the same time as the municipal election came along.

Interestingly, the politicians who supported the single-tier option were almost all defeated in November 2000. On the other hand, the mayor of Mono, John Creelman, who staunchly rejected the City of Dufferin model, was re-elected and subsequently named county warden. And for now, at least, Dufferin's simmering rivalries lie quietly in abeyance.

Orangeville on the Rise

In 1863, a year after Orangeville's leaders passed a resolution that would eventually result in the formation of Dufferin County, the village of Orangeville was incorporated. Orange Lawrence, who died two years before, is nonetheless credited with founding the town. He lived there for 18 years, having arrived in 1843 from Connecticut by way of Halton. Shortly thereafter he built a second mill in the village known for a time as Grigg's Mills in recognition of its first mill owner.

In 1851, Chisholm Miller followed Orange Lawrence's directions and drafted plans for the town's south side. Following existing property lines, he laid out narrow winding streets on land, much of it once owned by Lawrence, between Broadway and the Townline.

Five years later, J. Stoughton Dennis put together a very different plan for Orangeville's north side. Jesse Ketchum III, one of Dufferin's founding fathers and the man who owned land in this part of town, requisitioned its broad, straight street pattern. His choice of the name Broadway for the main thoroughfare and his use of numbered streets and avenues, all borrowed from New York City, reflect Ketchum's bold hopes for Orangeville. He set up Broadway as the commercial sector. Rather than living accommodations, the space above main-street businesses was reserved for tailors and lawyers, accountants and other purveyors of services necessary in a growing Upper Canada town. Known for a time as "The Town of Trees," Orangeville has Ketchum to thank for much of its greenery as well. He planted dozens of trees, many of which still grace Orangeville's historic centre.

Ketchum's local pedigree was as long as Lawrence's was short. His father, Jesse, was a philanthropic temperance leader and member of the Upper Canada Legislature. Moreover, he was Seneca Ketchum's nephew. When Seneca arrived in the community of Purple Hill, next door to today's Orangeville, Jesse Ketchum III's very colourful uncle was already almost 60 years old. Though never ordained by the Church of

Orange Lawrence, Orangeville's founding father and namesake.

Blue Moon Country Store north of Orangeville, formerly S.S. 6 Mono, known as Mono College.

Violet Hill's Granny Taught Us How, a restored Orange Lodge.

England, he came to preach and was licensed as the "Missionary of the Township of Mono" in 1830 by Bishop John Strachan himself.

Seneca died in 1850 when he was almost 80 years old. Without children, he left his considerable land holdings to the church. However, his brother Jesse disputed these instructions, eventually paid off other heirs and turned the land over to his son Jesse Ketchum III. For this reason, the younger Ketchum came to play a key role in Orangeville's coming of age.

Orangeville's name was not, as many people presume, connected with the Loyal Orange Lodge, an organization that was once a powerful and conservative force in Dufferin County. Nor was it the result of a choice between Newtonville and Orangeville that involved a bet to see if a whiskey bottle could travel safely over the rapids in the millrace. Instead, the record shows that at the christening of Orange Lawrence's mill, the mill manager's wife, Mary Newton, suggested the name Orangeville as a tribute to Orange Lawrence, the mill's owner and the town's first postmaster (who, ironically, was not an Orangeman).

Orangeville's elders clearly had a vision for their home. They set the stage by passing the resolution to form Dufferin County and seldom let up on their plans. Though Orangeville's Broadway never lived up to its famous namesake, the town fared well in comparison with its neighbours.

In 1871, the first locomotive owned by the Toronto, Grey & Bruce Railway (TG&B) steamed into this increasingly self-confident community. Orangeville's more suitable geography and, in all likelihood, its ability to woo railway officials, helped it out-compete its longtime commercial rival, Market Hill (Mono Mills), for the iron horse.

Some eight years later, in 1879, the Credit Valley Railway followed the TG&B's arrival. For a time, Orangeville had two railway stations and was a significant transportation hub. Then, in 1881, the courthouse, jail and registry office were built on Zina Street. Orangeville became the county town and has seldom looked back.

Today, with a population of over 25,000, while Shelburne has about 4,000 residents and Mono Mills less than 1,000, Orangeville continues to grow and prosper. Orangeville has matured into its role as county town. The seat of County Council, home to the completely refurbished Opera House and Dufferin's economic driver, Orangeville is, in the words of residents Laura Bird and her partner Javier Santamaria, "a flourishing, creative community that is both inspired and inspirational."

Mill Street, Orangeville, looking north.

SHELBURNE: IN FINE FIDDLE

In 1864, William Jelly left the village of Jellyby in Augusta Township and arrived at the southern terminus of the Toronto-Sydenham Road. An entrepreneur, he built a tavern and called it the British Canadian Hotel, though it was better known as Jelly's Tavern.

Soon after he opened his hotel, William set up a post office inside and became the first postmaster in Jelly's Corners, as Shelburne was first known.

As the village expanded, it outgrew the name Jelly's Corners. Its mostly Irish inhabitants suggested Tanderagee, to remember William Jelly's hometown in Northern Ireland. But the Canadian Parliament had a mind of its own and bestowed the name Shelburne on the community. The Earl of Shelburne had helped end hostilities between Britain, the United States and Canada.

A sleepy village virtually cut off from the world by a sea of trees, Shelburne found its fortunes changed when the railway came through, passing Hall's Corners by. As was so often the situation, a transportation route dictated the town's fate. In Shelburne's case, cheaper land and possibly some clever dealing meant the Toronto, Grey & Bruce Railway arrived in Shelburne in 1873 — amid much excitement. Finally, merchants could get their wares to market. This was certainly true for timber. Shelburne's largely untouched forest was now a valued commodity.

Shelburne's incorporation occurred in 1879, a full sixteen years after Orangeville became an independent municipality. William Jelly was its first reeve, a post he held from 1879 to 1900, with the exception of one three-year term. Though William wasn't the only famous Jelly in Shelburne, as founder and key political figure of the village, he is remembered as the "Father of Shelburne."

According to *An Atlas of Grey County*, by 1880, Shelburne had almost 1,000 inhabitants. It had eight general stores, two drug stores, several hotels, one steam gristmill, two steam sawmills, a foundry, tannery and a weekly newspaper — the *Free Press*. It had schools, churches, a railway and a bold, bright future. But fire would tarnish Shelburne's finery.

In 1884, a scant few months after the three-storied brick Royal Hotel opened for business, fire broke out and destroyed the new inn and all its street-level shops. For weeks, the entire block from Owen Sound Street to Jelly's Lane was a blackened mess. But with a will not uncommon in Ontario's pioneers, a new owner rebuilt the hotel and then sold it to William Jelly. However, the new Royal Hotel was not open for long. In 1886, fire once again wiped out the

Main Street, Shelburne, looking east, circa 1935.

Shelburne Municipal Offices.

entire block. And then, just two weeks later, a different fire destroyed the Irwin Brothers Cabinet Works, another prominent business in Shelburne. Amazingly, William Jelly built a third Royal Hotel and made it more luxurious than ever. With 50 guestrooms and an elegant dining room, the Royal Hotel served the community until 1920. By this time, fire-fighting services had improved throughout Dufferin County and one of the greatest threats to life and livelihood in early Ontario was no longer the curse it had once been.

As settlers arrived to clear the land and traffic increased on the Toronto-Sydenham (Owen Sound) Road, Shelburne experienced bursts of good fortune.

Its most famous event, the Canadian Open Old Time Championship Fiddle Contest, started as a one-evening affair in 1951. Every August since then, thousands of people from across the continent descend on the town, many bearing fiddles. They compete in one of the premier events of its kind anywhere while they enjoy Shelburne, a comfortable small town where it's impossible for residents and local farmers to stroll down Main Street without meeting up with neighbours and old friends.

Grand Valley's Infamous Moment

In this age of immediate communication, it's hard to find anyone without a service or a machine that will answer the telephone. But if you call the municipal offices in Grand Valley, there's a chance the phone will ring busy. This apparent lack of concern with the outside world seems to have always characterized Grand Valley, Dufferin's most westerly and third-largest town.

First known as Joice's Corners, the settlement became Luther Village when its post office opened in 1860. But no one seemed satisfied with that name. There were attempts to rename it Manasseh and Little Toronto, and a Colonel Higginbotham from Guelph even tried to relocate the town and call it Wellington. Grand Valley didn't stick until a nearby mill received some recognition for its Grand Valley Brand flour and townspeople opted for this pretty name.

Not incorporated until 1897, when its population reached the obligatory 750, it was never in the race to become the county town, so neither Orangeville nor Shelburne viewed Grand Valley as competition. As Adelaide Leitch wrote in *Into the High County*, "They didn't have the furious, mud-slinging political battles of Orangeville, or the upsurge of growth and jealousy of Shelburne." Instead, the town has always been pleasantly quiet…at least almost always.

For back on May 31, 1985, Grand Valley was anything but peaceful. That was the day when Dufferin's largest tornado hit town and stories about Grand Valley filled the airwaves. At 4:30 in the afternoon on an otherwise sunny Friday, the skies darkened and residents could be excused if they believed the wrath of God was upon them.

Doug Hunter was on his way to meet "Tillie" Mathilda McIntyre, a relative who'd just arrived from Scotland. In one of those weird twists of fate, Doug is lucky he didn't leave any earlier to meet his 76-year-old cousin. If he had, he too might have been a statistic on the six o'clock news. Tillie died that day. So did 50-year-old Barry Wood of East Luther. While the twister destroyed the house Tillie was visiting, it picked up Barry and his truck and hurled them off the road.

The tornado touched down at random in Dufferin County, but it seemed to concentrate on a few unlucky targets. Earl and Grace Dodds had two farms all but

Main Street, Grand Valley, looking north, circa 1910.

Amaranth Street house, Grand Valley, destroyed by the 1985 tornado along with 101 other buildings.

wiped out. It levelled Mono Plaza, just north of Orangeville and, reaching more than 500 km/h, its winds destroyed some 8 homes and 12 barns in Mono and severely damaged 25 more.

But the demon saved its greatest fury for Grand Valley. With miraculous precision, the eye of the storm travelled down the entire length of Amaranth Street, wiping out 101 buildings and damaging 200 more. It ripped out 89 hydro poles and uprooted hundreds of trees. Incredibly, Tillie and Barry were the only people killed on that never-to-be-forgotten Friday, but the tornado's minute-long rampage transformed a quiet street into a disaster area.

The *Weekend Banner* on June 14 described the scene: "Rubble was strewn for blocks, cars were blown away like they were plastic, homes looked as if they had

The Grand River winds its way under the Brooklyn Bridge and through the heart of Grand Valley.

The Olde Stanton Store, Stanton.

exploded from the inside." Wind levelled Grand Valley's Town Hall and Public Library. It injured 70 people and, in what seemed a wink of an eye, left hundreds homeless.

Today, all the new houses on Amaranth Street won't surprise newcomers. There is little physical evidence of what happened on that fateful day. But the people who lived there in 1985 recall the horror. They remember the sound and the fury in the eye of that deadly twister and hope it was a once-in-a-lifetime experience.

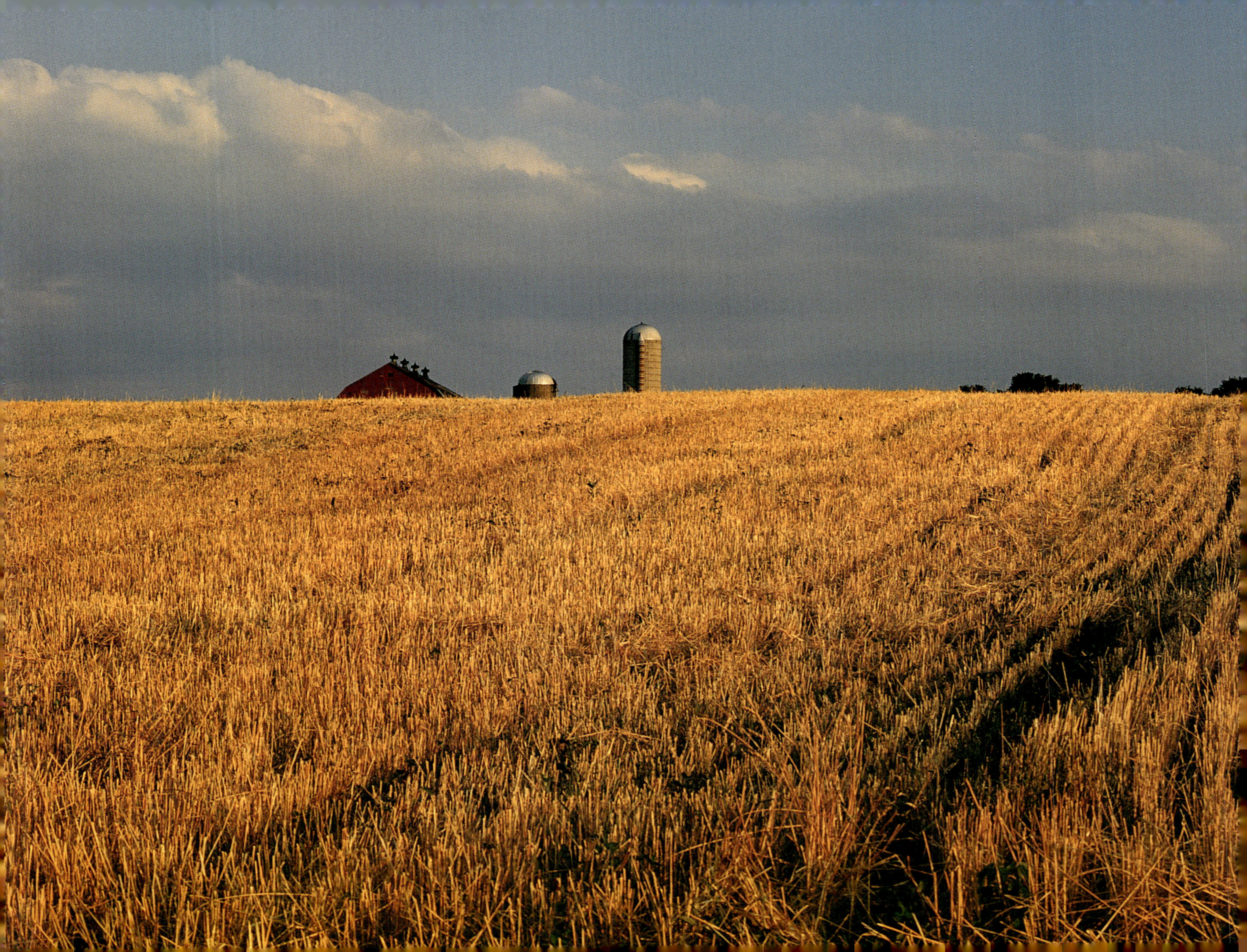

CHAPTER FIVE

Still the Mainstay of Dufferin's Economy

"Our family has been in Dufferin for three generations. We're here still because of the good soil,
lots of good friends close by, and the fact that it still is country."
—*Gerry and Tricia Reid and their family operate a mixed farm in Mono.*

"I thought it was too good a farm to go for gravel, so I fought it and won for a time."
—*Cooper Bath, born in 1916 in Toronto, potato farmer, Mono.*

Mel and Irene Tupling planted four acres of potatoes when they first began farming near Honeywood in 1944. Almost 60 years later, their son Bert, his wife and two sons have about 1,000 acres in potatoes at any given time. They store up to 18 million Sheppardies, Yukon Golds and especially Superiors in climate-controlled buildings, and employ as many as 22 workers during their busy season. With $7 million and their lives invested in farming, the future looks good for the Tuplings: the boys will take over the farm and the entire family makes its living from the land. Bert clearly enjoys what he does. He says, "We don't take fancy holidays. Instead, we get our kicks from replacing a 180-horsepower tractor with a 260."

The Tuplings, like all of Dufferin County's farmers, have some very hearty settlers to thank for opening up the land and starting Dufferin's late and highly condensed agricultural revolution. Finding no shorelines to fish, few quarries to mine and a fickle climate, the earliest settlers avoided Dufferin's high hills. So when land-hungry Irish immigrants arrived in the 1830s and 1840s, there was land for them up high, on top of the Niagara Escarpment.

These pioneers from Northern Ireland were unaware of the challenges that lay ahead when the Crown Lands

Home is just over the next hill.

Barn raising at Glenn Cross, circa 1906.

Department assigned them property in the high county. In addition to the typical hardships, settlers discovered that after climbing Caledon Mountain, the roads quickly faded into tracks and soon disappeared altogether.

Men often headed out into the hills in advance of their families. If possible they would stay with a neighbour until they'd put up a shanty. But before building, a settler would have to select a site, clear it, level it, cut the logs and haul them into place. Only then would he turn to his neighbours to "ask hands" for "the raising." But having a house didn't make life easy. The first year the family would tear up the ground between stumps. They'd sow seed grain by hand and hope an errant frost didn't compromise their primary source of food.

During Dufferin's settlement period, pioneers had to clear several acres, build a home and pay for the land before they received the deed. In this fashion, the landscape opened up little by little, but ten or more years would pass before tree roots had rotted sufficiently so

Honeywood, where farmers enjoy fertile Honeywood silt loam.

they could be removed. In the meantime, homesteaders worked the land between and around what were often huge stumps from ancient cherry, maple, beech, pine and basswood trees. Fortunately, the land was generous in those early days. Harvests were bountiful on the previously unbroken soil, and despite the hardships, Dufferin's settlers thrived.

In less than 50 years they not only established farms, they also built towns to service their agricultural, social and spiritual needs. Each had hotels and schools, churches, blacksmith shops, sawmills and a post office. Villages that are little more than a crossroads today were bustling, happening places.

Take Whittington, at the corner of Amaranth's 2nd Line and 15 Sideroad, for example. A lowland Scot, Robert Bowsfield, bought the land at this junction for $25 in 1857. Inspired by the rags-to-riches story of Dick Whittington, Lord Mayor of London, and his famous cat, Bowsfield erected a hotel in 1858 and called it Whittington House, from which the settlement derived

Melancthon Township.

Oil rig, Hockley Valley.

Wool and whiskey, Berwick's Store, Shelburne.

its name. But he didn't stop there. He also built a general store and a post office. There was a schoolhouse that became a Methodist church in 1873, and a cheese factory, and for a time during the 1860s, Whittington was a stop on the stagecoach run between Brampton and Owen Sound. Whittington even had its own orchestra between 1916 and 1919.

By the late 1800s, settlement in Dufferin had pretty well caught up with surrounding areas. A typical 100-acre mixed farm had a few cows and chickens, a number of pigs, workhorses and maybe some sheep. Farmers grew oats and hay to feed their livestock and wheat became flour. If the year was a good one, they might have something left over to sell for cash. Vegetable gardens and fruit trees received loving attention. They provided the bulk of the food that would maintain farm families over the long, cold winter.

Farmers were keen to find some relief from their relentless work. In *The Story of Albion*, Esther Heyes

device gave way to steam-powered threshers that were hauled from farm to farm by their owners. When one barn was almost threshed out, a special whistle signal summoned the next farmer on the route. He'd bring his team, pick up and then fill the water tank so it was ready and waiting when the threshing team arrived.

Gristmills and threshers weren't the only innovations that catapulted farmers from Dufferin's abbreviated agricultural revolution into the industrial one. Cream separators, hay loaders and manure spreaders also helped. They preceded the two inventions that really changed farming. Though hydroelectric power arrived in Dufferin before 1910, few farmers could either afford or have access to it until after the Second World War. Electricity allowed indoor plumbing—a toilet in the house and running water in the barn. Tractors also appeared in the county as early as 1911, but once again cost and availability were problems until after the war. By the 1950s, however, most farms had

Tipling's Blacksmith Shop, Shelburne.

writes, "It took most of the previous evening's hours to produce enough flour for the next day's needs, and the overworked men vowed they would rather chop down trees in the forest all day long than grind one bushel of grain." Farmers would line up for days at a gristmill and were quick to try any new technology that might save time, thereby allowing them to expand their operations. Horse-powered threshing machines replaced hand flailing to separate chaff from the grain. This

Steam threshers like this one, circa 1900, travelled from farm to farm to remove the straw and chaff from the grain.

Energy from the wind.

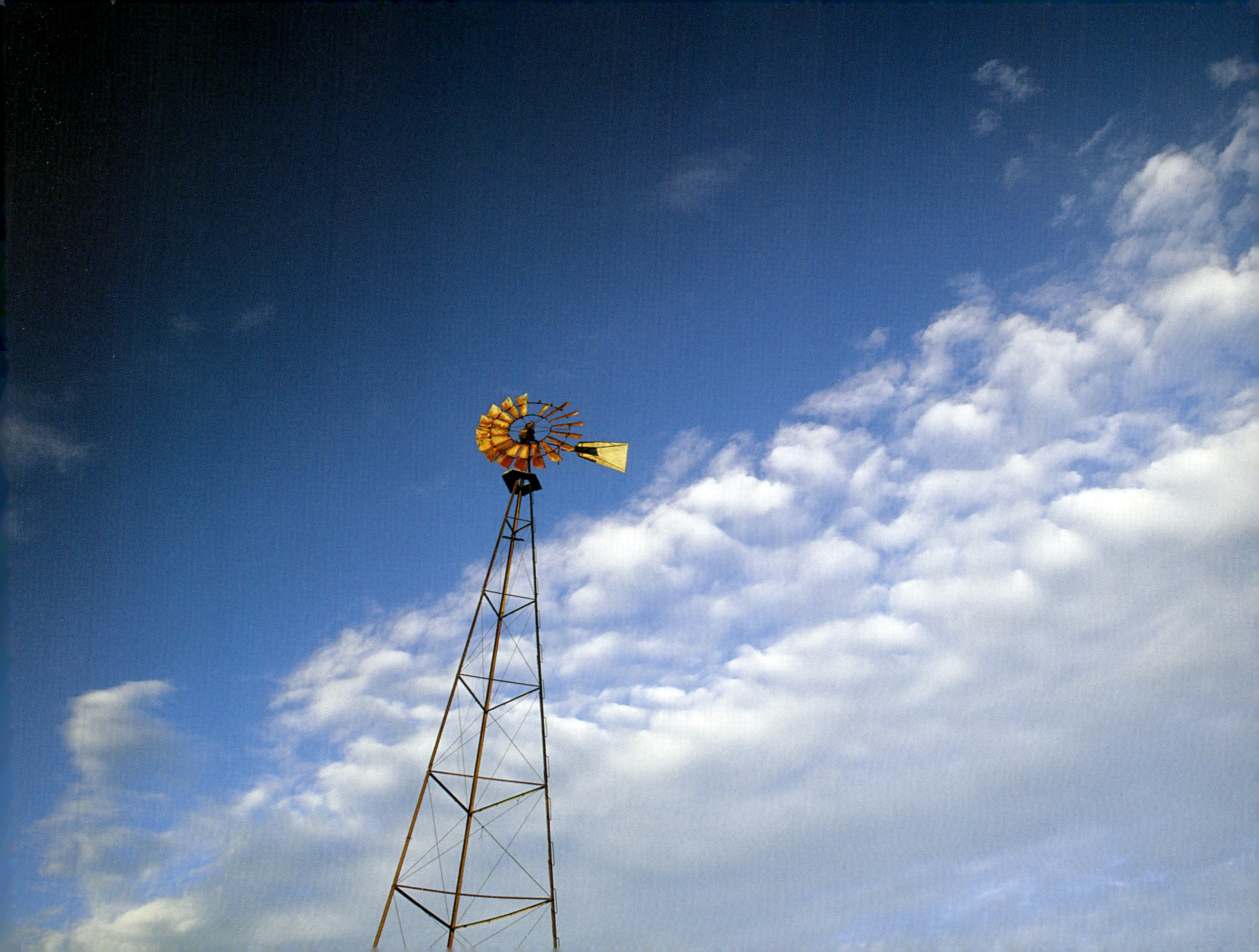

Rows of canola straw snake across fields in East Garafraxa.

electricity and a tractor. Cooper Bath, who began farming in Mono in the 1940s, recalls retiring his seven Belgian horses after getting his first tractor in the early 1950s. These technologies allowed farmers to work even more land. Mixed farms were still the standard, but a trend toward larger and more specialized operations was underway.

Dairy farms and then feedlots and cow-calf operations replaced mixed farms during the 1960s and 1970s. Then, in the 1980s, when soaring interest rates put the majority of feedlots out of business, many farmers turned to cash cropping. Doug Gear, a longtime farmer in East Garafraxa, watched Dufferin change. He recalls when every farm up and down the road had some livestock. Now, he notes, there is hardly any.

It wasn't only the vagaries of raising livestock that convinced farmers they should turn to cash cropping; new varieties of soybeans and corn that thrive in the frosty high country came along as well. Canola, a relatively new oilseed that's related to mustard, loves Dufferin's cool climate. In early July, the pungently aromatic fields of intense yellow flowers brighten Dufferin's patchwork of green hay and barley crops. Canola adds colour, texture and a source of income to the landscape.

Agricultural Representative Harold Dorrance on Dufferin's first tractor, in 1911.

Milk Bar, Shelburne, circa 1940.

Despite the risk of a July frost or, more accurately, because of it, few places produce better potatoes than Dufferin. It has an ideal climate for "padedahs," as they're known locally, and Honeywood silt loam blesses the potato belt that straddles parts of Mulmur and Melancthon. As farmers around Shelburne and Honeywood realized their land was ideally suited to growing potatoes, they too gave up their livestock.

These days, if you travel north from Shelburne during the summer or fall, you'll see specialized potato-harvesting equipment criss-crossing wide-open fields that rival the prairies for flatness.

Bert and Pat Tupling and their two sons farm over 2,000 acres, owning just under half of the land. They store, package and haul their own spuds as well as those produced on some of the smaller potato farms. Even though the Tupling's gross income exceeds $2 million,

Croquet in Bowling Green.

Butcher shop, Shelburne, circa 1920.

AER Motors windmills for sale in Shelburne.

Common garden in Shelburne (Jeremiah Brundige, 1910).

their operation isn't the largest in the area. That distinction belongs to the Downey brothers.

Together with the Vanderzaags and Rutledges — other big potato families — the Tuplings, Downeys and other smaller producers compete each year to see who can produce the most potatoes from an acre of land. The winner joins the 500-bushel club, so called because in the 1950s, when the contest began, a 500-bushel-acre was extreme. These days, as a result of new varieties and higher agricultural inputs, more than 750 bushels of french fries-in-waiting are usually coaxed from the winning acre.

Most grocery stores carry Dufferin potatoes. They are also turned into potato chips, french fries and soup. Potatoes and the Honeywood silt loam they grow in put Dufferin firmly on Ontario's agricultural map. They also make this part of Melancthon and Mulmur true farm country, since the land is worth more for agriculture than it is for urban development.

Another agricultural trend taking hold in Dufferin involves supplying niche markets. Dave Besley, traditionally a dairy farmer, now raises ewes or, as he calls them, "yoes." Dave claims sheep farming is the fastest-growing sector around and for good reason: you can make pretty good money at it.

Bill and Diane French own Lennox Farm, one of a handful of large-scale rhubarb operations in the province. Cultivating prized Honeywood silt loam, Bill and Diane also harvest 70 acres of peas and another 10 acres of brussel sprouts and they're packaging their own Taste of Spring brand of rhubarb syrup and jam.

On the Mono-Amaranth Townline, Jim Collins plants almost 200 acres of spinach on Gordon Gillespie's old farm. Over in Mulmur, John and Isabel Ireland grow about a dozen varieties of apples. John

Agriculture is still the biggest business in Dufferin.

Mulmur Township.

admits the climate isn't ideal for fruit, but that means they haven't much competition nearby. They sell 80 percent of their crop, as well as cider and honey, at the farm gate.

In operation at its current location near Orangeville since 1997, Woolwich Diary is owned by Tony and Olga Dutra. At last count, Woolwich commanded 60 percent of the goat cheese market in Canada. Supplying Woolwich with the 20 million litres of goat milk the company requires annually to produce 2 million pounds of cheese has presented local farmers with yet another opportunity.

More a way of life than an industrial sector, farming continues to drive Dufferin's local economy. Terry Sullivan, a former agricultural representative for Dufferin, says, "Agriculture has been the backbone of the community." Though businesses such as FernBrook Spring Water, Johnson Controls Inc., Symplastics Ltd., Greening Donald Co. Ltd. and others provide good jobs, Dufferin is still farm country. Like so many others, Bert Tupling can't see himself doing anything else. "It's hard for me in my life," says Bert, "to get out of the tractor seat."

A Trio of Fall Fairs

A Dufferin institution that, like farming, has changed over time but not gone away is its agricultural fairs. Each fall, fairs in Orangeville, Shelburne and Grand Valley attract thousands of residents and visitors. Many of them, admits Earl Dodds, Orangeville's fairground manager, come to watch the demolition derby. But people still love to see the cows, sheep and

Bill French, Lennox Farm.

Many of Dufferin's farmers became cash croppers in the 1980s.

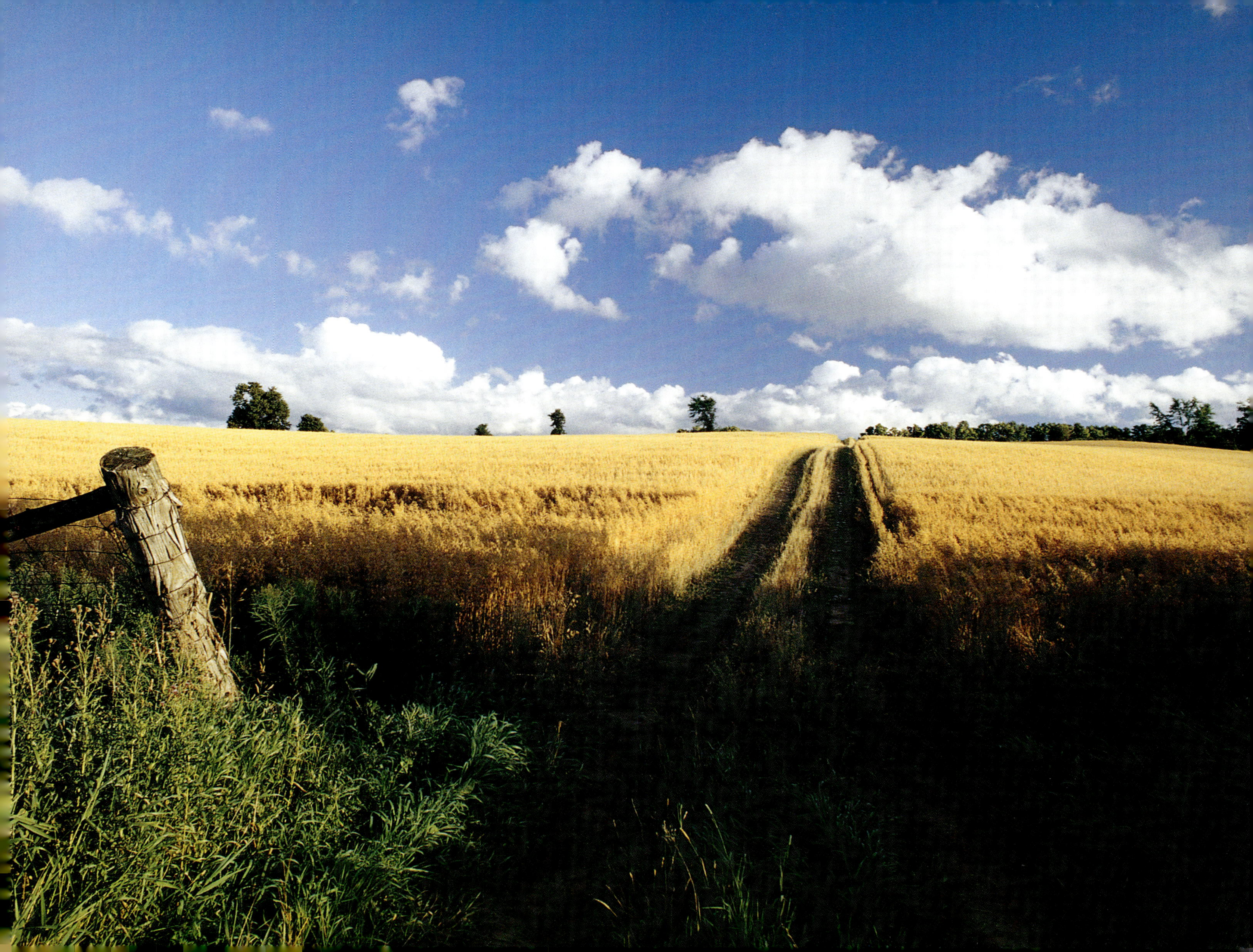

Orangeville Fall Fair, mid-1960s, on the original fairgrounds where WalMart now sits.

horses, just as they did way back in the 1850s when Orangeville's first fair took place. They look at the exhibits of grain and vegetables, and admire prize-winning quilts, jams, jellies and pumpkins so huge they cave in on themselves.

Rural fairs are great places to educate people about farm life and food. "Many city kids think chocolate milk comes from a brown cow," says Earl. So all Grade Three students in Dufferin are given an agri-food education day at the fair in their respective communities.

The Orangeville Fall Fair is Dufferin's largest, especially since 1997 when it moved from the old racetrack in town (where the Wal-Mart now resides) to its new home on Mono's 5 Sideroad. Each Labour Day weekend, over 20,000 people pass through the gates at Orangeville's new fairgrounds.

But Orangeville is by no means the only stop on the fall fair circuit. Two weeks later, Shelburne puts on a show of its own. Smaller than the Orangeville fair, Shelburne's event shares many features. The demolition derby is a big draw, so too is the heavy horse pull. But the 134-year-old Shelburne fair's greatest moment eclipsed these events. Back in 1959, Prime Minister John Diefenbaker attended the Shelburne Fall Fair, attracting a huge crowd of curious onlookers. Jim Montgomery was there. Dryly, he recalls, "It was quite an occasion to have the P. M. attend."

Last but not least in the trio is the fair in Grand Valley. The earliest fairs took place on "The Commons" between Gier Street and the river in Luther Village (now Grand Valley), and the East Luther Agricultural Society (precursor to the Grand Valley Agricultural Society) put it on. Back in those days the featured event was a horserace. It began at the bridge and had its exciting finish at Main Street.

Grand Valley Fall Fair's Heavy Horse Show.

Now, for three days over the third weekend in September, Grand Valley comes alive with dozens of events ranging from the 4-H Dairy Club Show to a Horseshoe Pitch Contest to a pre-school award for arts and crafts. Ellen Bryan, the fair's treasurer, puts in hours pulling the fair together. When asked how many

The 4-H Goat Show at the Grand Valley Fall Fair.

Dufferin County display at the CNE, circa 1925.

their land and built their homes, but, as the story goes, the trees were so dense, they didn't discover each other's presence until a year after they'd settled.

Nonetheless, by 1900, pioneers had felled most of Dufferin's trees, sometimes with dire consequences. Terry Sullivan, an agricultural representative in Dufferin County throughout the 1980s and 1990s, says that a lot of the hillier land in Mono should never have been cleared. (Maybe settlers should have paid more heed to the resident Natives, since one possible derivation of the name Mono is the Native for "let it be." More likely, however, it came from *mono*, the Spanish word for monkey.) Without a tree cover, the sandy soils were free to drift. And drift they did. Born in 1909, Shelly Anderson can point out old sand dunes that line Airport Road just north of the Hockley Road. He recalls when wind blew the sand so hard the roads had to be ploughed in summer. Over in Amaranth, so few people it takes to run a fair like Grand Valley's, her response likely doesn't differ from those who organized the first Grand Valley fair 130 years ago. Ellen replies, "We never get as many as we need!" The large crowds that enjoy Dufferin's fall fairs indicate country folk will continue to organize these events and thereby keep agriculture alive and well for some time to come.

HEALING THE LANDSCAPE

In 1823, two of Mono's earliest families—the Turnbulls and the Henrys—arrived at almost the same time and in almost the same location. They cleared

The Orangeville Fall Fair.

Dufferin is known for its many Christmas tree farms.

trees escaped farmers' axes that beavers were wiped out and had to be reintroduced in the 1960s.

Trees were replanted to anchor the sandy soils in parts of Mono. Some of this reforested land is privately owned. But a good portion is part of an extensive system of county and township forests. Dufferin County has a total of 1,050 hectares of municipal forest and the Mono Forest covers another 187 hectares. In combination, these wooded areas have helped combat soil erosion in Dufferin.

Trees are also central to a local industry: Christmas tree farming. Shelly Anderson was one of Mono's original tree farmers. He first planted seedlings in Mono in 1929, but it wasn't until the 1940s that he realized there was a dollar to be made in trees. Never ones to do things halfway, Shelly and his wife, Elsie, also entered their Christmas trees at the Royal Winter Fair. Elsie's entry was the Grand Champion in 1956, the competition's first year, and the Andersons went on to compete for 27 consecutive years, winning 15 grand championships and 13 reserve championships. In 1987, Shelly was named the Christmas Tree Farmer of the Year and Mono was firmly on the map as a place to get your tannebaum.

The Besley boys break in a new combine.

An Archaeological Wonder

Dufferin farmers may not be surprised if there's a frost in July, but nothing prepared them for what turned up during the drought of 1887. It was so hot and dry that year that the swamp on William "Kitley Bill" Jelly's farm at Bowling Green in Amaranth dried up. Even the *Amaranthus*, or pigweed, after which Amaranth Township is likely named, was feeling the drought. Desperate to find water, Bill took to scraping out his slough. Down and down he went. And though he never reached his goal, Bill hit paydirt nonetheless. Just as his wife was calling him into supper, his scraper caught hold of what Bill mistook for a root. Digging deeper, he uncovered an enormous rib bone. Convinced he'd found the remains of no ordinary animal, Bill and his son dug on, pulling out several more bones before darkness forced them to give up their excavation.

That night the much-needed rain began. Several days later, when the downpour ended, the slough was full, their quarry buried once again. Patiently, they waited. Then, two years later, another drought allowed the digging to recommence. What they unearthed was half the skeleton of a mastodon, including its 8-foot tusks and several teeth weighing 14 pounds each. The Jellys had uncovered the remains of an animal that had roamed the hills some 10,000 years before and stood 11 feet tall at its withers. Bill sold the bones to his cousin John for the princely sum of $1,500. John put the "Amaranth Mastodon" to work. He displayed it in Shelburne, charging viewers ten cents for a peek, and then he took the skeleton and toured country fairs. Wherever the Amaranth Mastodon went it was the hit of the show.

The Amaranth Mastodon and John Kelly, circa 1890.

What happened to Bowling Green's famous skeleton? No one knows for sure. John sold it for $3,000 and its new owners stored it until 1915, when it appeared at the Canadian National Exhibition. Then it was reportedly seen in California, Wisconsin and Minnesota before disappearing forever.

The rolling hills of Mulmur.

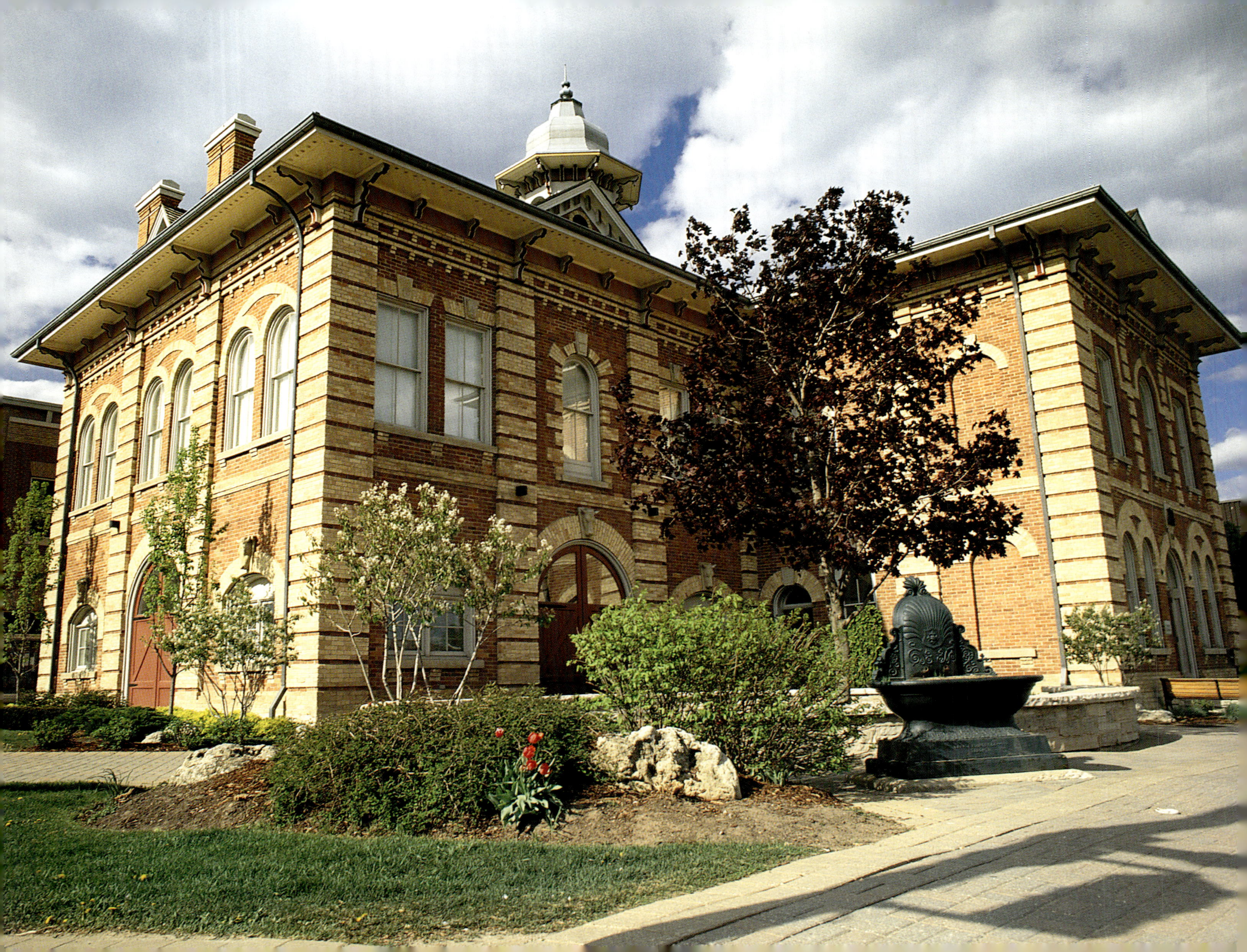

CHAPTER SIX

A Hotbed of Culture

"Dufferin County is country living at its best. The sense of community spirit is a perfect backdrop for the incredible natural beauty and culture of the area. In a matter of minutes you can experience the spectacular settings and hiking trails as well as an impressive array of theatre, art, history and musical events."
—*Nancy Frater, bookstore owner, community leader, Orangeville.*

"Generally, I'm a hermit. That's one of the reasons I came here. So it was a surprise. All of a sudden there were all these other artists."
—*Hugh Russel, full-time sculptor, Mulmur.*

"If we offered a performance of *Wingfield Farms* at two A.M. on a Sunday morning during an ice storm," says Theatre Orangeville's artistic director, David Nairn, "we'd still sell it out." The popularity of the Wingfield plays in Dufferin County shouldn't be a surprise since much of the material used in Dan Needles' one-man, multi-character shows can be traced back to the 1970s when he lived on the 7th Line of Mono and edited the *Shelburne Free Press & Economist.*

In order to fill space and perk up an otherwise ordinary small-town newspaper, Dan created a column that allowed him to talk about what was really happening in town without naming names. It took the form of a weekly letter to the editor penned by Walt Wingfield. Walt, a fictitious newcomer to the community, had given up the big job in the big city to farm the old Fisher place a ways down the 7th Line. In the column, Mono became Persephone Township and Shelburne appeared as Larkspur.

The transition from newspaper column to nationally touring stage production has been a huge success. But no other community embraces the shows like Dufferin County. Old timers and newcomers alike turn up in droves to laugh and sometimes cry as Rod Beattie, the star of all the Wingfield plays, pokes fun at their everyday lives.

Orangeville Theatre stages its popular productions in the Opera House
— "on Broadway."

Performance at the Shelburne Opera House.

Carnegie Library, Grand Valley, destroyed by the 1985 tornado.

These performances may be Theatre Orangeville's biggest sellers, but they are by no means the only shows that draw crowds into one of the loveliest concert halls in rural Ontario. Originally built in 1875, the Town Hall Opera House seats 276 and occupies much of the second floor of Orangeville's municipal building on Broadway. It was a fixture for Orangeville theatre-goers at the turn of the last century. But use dropped off and by the 1960s the hall was at risk of demolition. Luckily for Orangeville, the Ontario government approved an application to rebuild the Opera House…and Jim Betts came to town.

Jim, a newcomer by anyone's definition, made his mark by proposing and then following through on a plan to prevent the new Opera House from becoming a white elephant. He created a professional theatre company to entertain people of all ages throughout the summer months. In 1994, the doors opened and Threatre Orangeville was born.

The artistic director for five years, Jim often used local talent to create what were occasionally world-premiere performances. He also focussed on a kid's program. Jim received numerous awards, writing many of the family-oriented plays performed by Threatre Orangeville. He also saw several of his protégés use Theatre Orangeville as a stepping stone to bigger things.

For instance, in 1997, the Theatre Orangeville Young Singers out-performed 150 choirs to become part of *Joseph and the Amazing Technicolor Dream Coat*, the Andrew Lloyd Webber musical. For three months the choir performed alongside Donny Osmond at Toronto's Elgin Theatre. A young star, Tamara Hope of Shelburne, used the experience she gained by performing in Theatre Orangeville's *The Shooting of Dan McGrew* to launch an award-winning acting career that takes her to Los Angeles on occasion. And the list goes on, with local youths moving between Theatre Orangeville productions and shows such as the CBC's *Wind at My Back* or Treehouse Television's popular show *Ants in Your Pants*.

Orangeville High School, built in 1884, destroyed by fire in 1948.

After Jim moved on, David Nairn took up the challenge. David kept the children's program alive. In 2001, he offered a world premiere of a musical version of *Little Women*. Jim Betts wrote the music and lyrics for the production, while a local writer, Nancy Early, adapted the book for the stage, and several of the actors heralded from the community.

But not all at Theatre Orangeville is as Jim Betts left it. Since there are about a dozen summer theatres within an hour's drive of Orangeville, David transformed Theatre Orangeville into the only professional company in the area with a winter program. Banking on its growing reputation for quality performances, Theatre Orangeville's winter schedule now begins in September and runs until May.

When Theatre Orangeville is between productions, the Orangeville Concert Association may offer classical or jazz performances, or Orangeville Music Theatre might run through final rehearsals for a musical starring local amateur talent. You might catch a folk singer as part of the Headwaters Acoustic Music Society's Concert Series or a local service club's fundraising event.

Then, for seventeen days in early October each year, the Opera House becomes one of several dozen venues for the Headwaters Arts Festival. Starting in 1996, this celebration of arts and culture in Dufferin County and its neighbouring communities features art exhibitions, studio tours, music, theatre, literary readings and an interactive art component for kids. By bringing arts patrons into the area, the Arts Festival makes it possible for local artists to spend more and more time at home doing what they love.

Laurie McGaw's studio is a popular stop on the Headwaters Studio Tour that takes place during the Arts Festival. An illustrator and portrait artist, Laurie is best known for her illustrations in the book *Polar the Titanic Bear*. There are more than 650,000 copies of this book, available in five languages, in people's homes, all bearing Laurie's distinctive drawings. She came to Mulmur in 1990 and says the peace and quiet of her new home feed her creativity.

Al Pace, a full-time potter who arrived in the Hockley Valley in 1987, opens his studio to the public most days but puts in extra effort while the Arts Festival is on. Al recognizes that his ability to make a living at his craft depends on Dufferin's growing reputation as a beautiful place where visitors will find fine art and see artists hard at work.

Farmhouse Pottery, in the Hockley Valley

Toad Hole Studio, in Mulmur.

One of the first artists to come to Dufferin was Linda McLaren. An illustrator, Linda arrived in Amaranth Township in the 1960s. Soon thereafter she joined the Orangeville Art Group, Dufferin's longest-running art organization. Its first show was in 1969 when, according to Linda, "there weren't many opportunities to show artwork." The group's 100 members organize workshops and have added their show and sale to the Headwaters Arts Festival.

It's hard to say whether all the musicians, actors, writers, journalists and artists who call Dufferin home caused there to be so many art associations, book

Dufferin County Museum and Archives.

clubs, craft sales, literary readings, jam sessions, galleries and one of the best independent bookstores around — or whether the latter attracted the former. But the result is the same: Dufferin, despite being the quirky rural community depicted in the Wingfield series, is a hotbed of artistic talent.

And that talent is helped along by the Dufferin County Museum & Archives. This huge red and green barn and silo complex commands the landscape at the corner of Highway 89 and Airport Road. It is a popular location for art shows, gala openings and musical and literary performances. These events take place alongside the old flag stop from Crombie's Station, a two-storey log house and an Orange Hall rebuilt inside the 26,000-square-foot, climate-controlled "barn," and next door to the old Corbetton church that was moved to and then resurrected on the museum grounds. Most community museums end up in historic buildings. This sounds great but there is seldom enough space for all that a museum can be. After some heated debate, Dufferin County did things differently. The result is an amazing facility ideally suited to its use.

Wayne Townsend, the museum's curator since it opened in 1994, is as much a part of Dufferin County as are the artefacts he puts on display. Born in 1952 and raised in Monticello near the Luther Marsh, Wayne was in Grade 7 when hydro came to town and Grade 8 when his folks installed indoor plumbing. His non-stop stories about the life and times of Dufferin County feed the cultural community. Aided and abetted by black-Irish-humour-loving archivist Steve Brown, who oversees the astonishing array of information about the county, much of it computer indexed, the Dufferin County Museum and Archives hides its technical genius behind a charmingly rural facade.

Probably the best outlet for Dufferin's stories is *In the Hills* magazine. Published in Mono since 1994, this deliciously beautiful publication never runs out of material, writers, artists and photographers from the Headwaters area. A given issue might profile Oliver Apitius, a mandolin maker in Mulmur; feature the Dufferin Piecemakers Quilting Guild; celebrate one of Dufferin's amazing gardens; describe a prize herd of cattle; or talk about musicians such as Gene DiNovi or Eric Nagler, who each have homes in Dufferin County.

Part of the magazine's magic is its broad appeal. From the weekenders who find respite in a country

Woodside Lodge, dancehall, tourist cabins, park, swimming, at Hockley Road and 5th Line.

hideaway from their frenzied Bay Street or media jobs to seventh-generation Dufferin farmers, residents hang on to every issue of the magazine and refer back to them regularly.

But Dufferin's granddaddy of cultural events is, undoubtably, the Canadian Open Old Time Championship Fiddle Contest. It's so much a part of Shelburne that while he was editor of the *Shelburne*

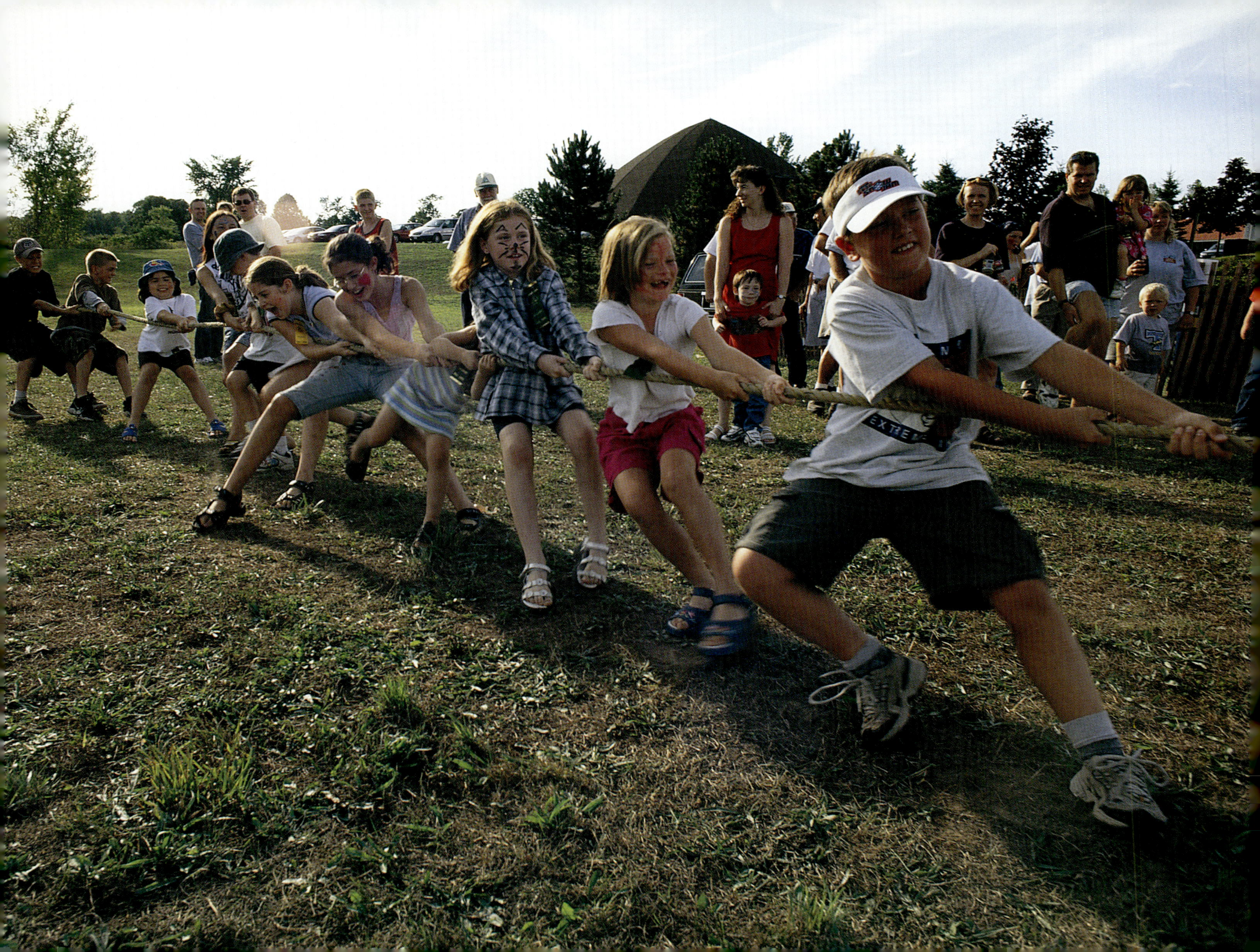

Free Press & Economist, Dan Needles complained that of the paper's 52 weekly issues, 26 were a warm-up for the Fiddle Contest and the other 26 were a wrap-up. All joking aside, Shelburne rallies around its major annual event that got its start over 50 years ago in 1951.

Fed up with fundraising events that took a huge amount of work but raised little money, and unwilling to hold lucrative games of chance, Cliff McIntosh, the manager of Shelburne's Royal Bank at the time, suggested Shelburne borrow the idea of a fiddle contest from a town he'd visited in western Canada. Fred Claridge, the publisher of Shelburne's newspaper, took the idea to a neighbour, weekender Don Fairbairn, who happened to host the CBC radio show *Neighbourly News*. Don got the CBC to broadcast the Saturday night finals (something the CBC did for 50 years) and, despite considerable scepticism, the Shelburne Rotary Club took on the event.

Forty-four contestants turned up that first year and the Fiddle Contest found a life of its own. In the early days, the dance that traditionally follows the final playoffs often ran into the wee morning hours. Dancers competed with fiddlers to see who could outlast whom. Over the years, the prize money increased and the contest attracted larger audiences and more competitors from further afield. In 2000, the contest's 50th anniversary, contestants competed for total prize money of over $11,000 and the competition included several classes not offered back in the earliest days. Now fiddlers over 65 years of age compete in their own category, as do the youngsters, some of whom are younger than nine.

Left: Mulmur's 150th birthday bash.

Brett Milley was one of the youngest stars of the 51st Canadian Open Fiddle Championship (2001).

Orangeville resident Chance Kellner took third prize in her first attempt at the contest in 1998. She was only eight. Though she's never repeated her original success, Chance says she likes participating in the contest. "The environment is really cool. I like listening. But it gets really tense when you have to perform." Stage fright, however, hasn't held this youngster back. Chance sometimes plays her fiddle as a busker. One time she worked the St. Lawrence Market in Toronto with a very talented step dancer Adrian Newcombe. Together the duo pulled in $240 for an hour's work. Chance is also a budding actor. She performed in Theatre Orangeville's world premiere of *Little Women*.

Mallory Holmes is another local fiddler. By the time Mallory was fifteen years old, the Shelburne resident had already made six appearances at the Fiddle Contest. She admits, however, that if she wants to be in the prize money she'll have to increase the 30 minutes she spends practising her fiddle to the three or four hours her fellow competitors manage on a daily basis.

For the contestants at the modern-day Fiddle Contest are no longer Saturday night amateurs. They are polished musicians. The contest measures their tempo, tone, style, technique and overall musical accuracy as they play reels or hoedowns, jigs and waltzes following a set of rules little changed since Cliff McIntosh drew them up back in 1951.

While Dufferin fiddlers have performed well over the years, it's really the entire community that is the winner. There are also a couple of particularly outstanding contributors. Vince Mountford competed the very first year. He grew up in Gooseville, a village that once existed on the Mono Centre Road and derived its intriguing name from the geese that used a nearby pond. His fiddling wasn't first class, but his story telling was. Organizers talked Vince into being the master of ceremonies, a role he fulfilled for 34 consecutive years. And Phyllis McDowell, a Shelburne resident, can't help but feel proud of her involvement in the fiddle contest. The daughter of a musician, Phyllis

Ed Huxtable, fiddler.

Duelling fiddles at the 50th Canadian Open Fiddle Championship (2000) in Shelburne.

Long-time fiddle accompanist Phyllis McDowell.

accompanied fiddlers on the piano at the very first contest and didn't give up her role until the year 2000. "The piano stool got to be pretty hard on my back," says Phyllis. Many of the best fiddlers that came to Shelburne—Graham Townsend, Al Cherny and Ed Gyurki—always requested that Phyllis accompany them in the final competition. In fact, Phyllis recalls that one year she played with eleven of the fifteen finalists, quite a compliment for any accompanist, especially one who doesn't read music.

What began in 1951 as a one-evening competition is now a four-day festival that involves all of Shelburne's service clubs and most residents. The Kinsmen Club organizes Saturday's parade. On Sunday, a pork barbecue follows a non-denominational community church service.

Fiddlefest, on Friday morning, involves a jam session for professional and amateur fiddlers who share their knowledge with fans. And money made by this musical event is spread around the entire community. Today's Canadian Open Old Time Championship Fiddle Contest may have lost some of the spontaneity of the old days, but it continues to bind Shelburne's residents together in a very special way.

Dufferin sculptor Hugh Russel, who bears some resemblance to Walt Wingfield of Dan Needles' plays, recently talked about his decade and a half in Dufferin County. Referring to the odd mix of old-time farmers and recently arrived artists like himself, he remarked, "They may not treat us as locals, but at least they treat us well."

Mansfield Outdoor Centre.

The Mansfield Ski Club.

Hockley Valley Resort.

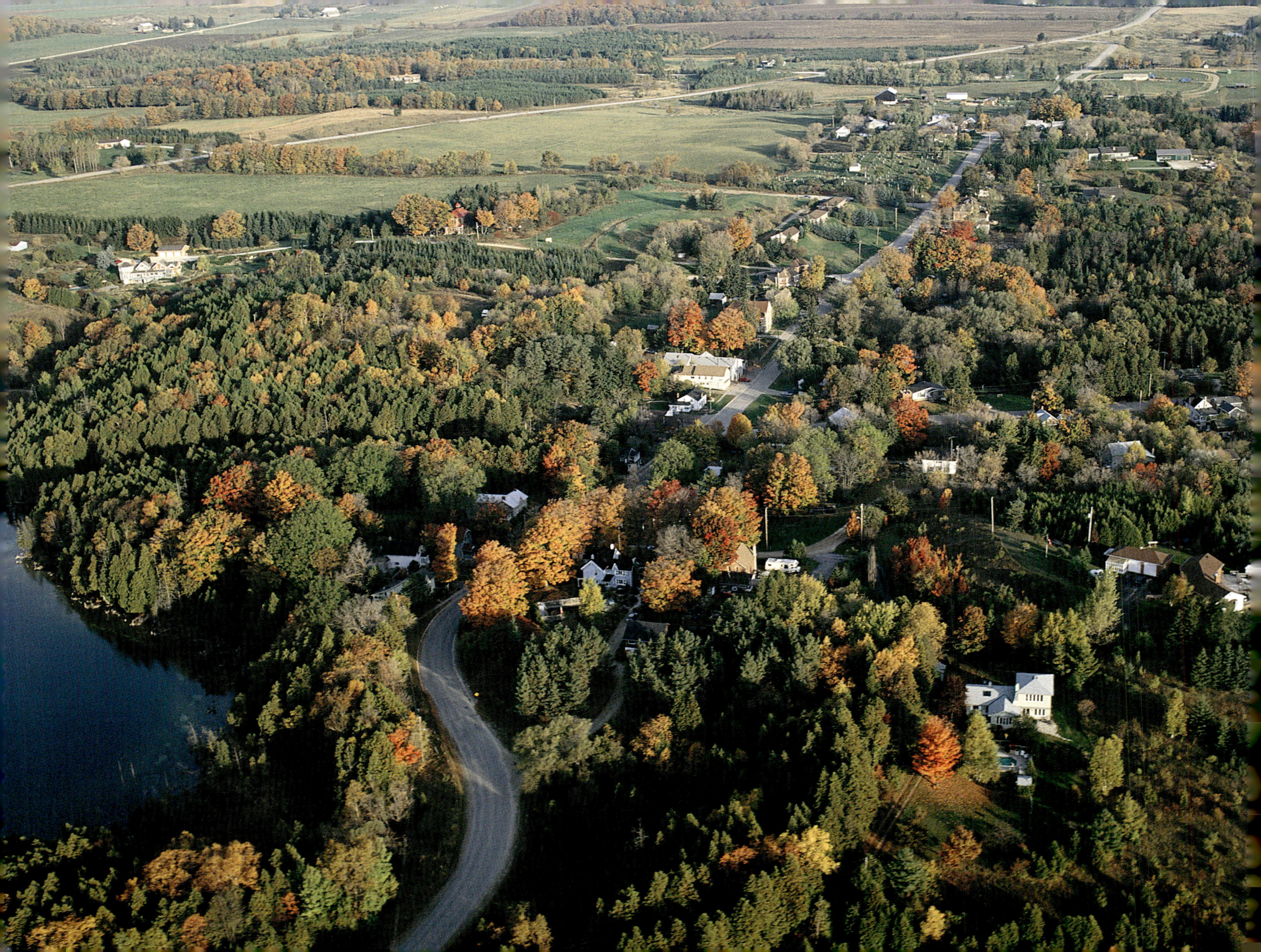

CHAPTER SEVEN

The Hollow at Horning's Mills

"It's an interesting coincidence that the place where my wife was born and we now live is at what's considered the safest place to live by those who believe in cataclysmic events."
—*Bruce Beach, who has built a nuclear fallout shelter using 42 old buses, of Horning's Mills.*

"What he instilled in us was that you took what life gave you."
—*Marjorie Milroy, T. R. and Elizabeth Huxtable's daughter, who spends her summers in Horning's Mills.*

Horning's Mills was not always a sleepy hollow. In fact, it outpaced Orangeville and Shelburne for a long time. In the late 1880s, it had two flour mills, two sawmills, a woollen mill, tannery, two general stores, two blacksmith shops, two shoemakers, two tailors, two wagon makers, a planing mill, hotel, undertaker and three churches. It was also home for the first of its long line of dreamers.

THE DREAM BEGINS: LEWIS HORNING

Pioneers arrived at the headwaters of the Pine River long before they settled in Shelburne and Orangeville. Having learned about the site from a surveyor's report, Lewis Horning purchased 2,500 acres of untouched wilderness in the vicinity. With a dream of creating his own village, this most unlikely pioneer from Hamilton rounded up all the tradesmen he would need to accomplish his goal, and in 1830, they set off for the bush. Before completing their journey they had cleared and built 26 miles of road to take them and their supplies high atop the Niagara Escarpment and some 40 miles beyond the nearest settlement.

Of considerable financial means, Lewis was an accomplished outdoorsman. He was also a consummate dreamer despite his 63 years of age, two marriages and 15 children. And his vision was strong, strong enough to withstand most, but not all, as it turned out, that Upper Canada's frontier would throw at him.

By 1838, Horning's Mills was well on its way to becoming a bustling community, but an unprecedented

Horning's Mills.

James Huxtable's mill, in Horning's Mills.

tragedy interrupted the town's bright progress. Returning from a day spent assisting friends, Lewis Horning learned that four village children were missing. An intense search ensued but no evidence could be found of Lewis' 9-year-old son or the two daughters and a son (aged 16, 14 and 9 respectively) of one of Lewis' employees. The villagers discovered no garments or fabric. They unearthed no evidence of a struggle and became convinced that rather than wild animals, Natives must be the culprits.

Relations with the local Natives became strained as townsfolk observed their former allies, hoping for signs of the children. There were many leads from missionaries, trappers and hunters. Some reported having seen the children. But each time the villagers followed up a clue, nothing could be found. One particularly friendly Native was suspected of alerting the children's captors to the villagers' search efforts. His unwillingness to accept a bribe, even a very generous one, however, lessened suspicions, but then he agreed that in return for Lewis' gold watch he would provide the coveted information. Sadly, according to an account prepared by Lewis Horning's grandson, he failed to keep his promise, claiming that death awaited him if he gave away the whereabouts of the children.

The most concrete lead the villagers had involved reported sightings of two white girls and boys at a Native event on Manitoulin Island. Peter Horning travelled in disguise to check it out, but without success.

Then, nearly two years after the alleged kidnapping took place and when all hope had been lost, one of the children, Oliver Vanmear, now 11 years old, turned up in Toronto Township. Though apparently unharmed, he could shed little light on his misadventure. For, as Lewis' grandson reported, "Oliver Vanmear was foolish, having been afflicted from his birth…" In other words, Oliver was mentally challenged and this, according to published records, accounts for why the Natives discarded the boy, and also his inability to describe the events of the previous two years.

So the mystery was never solved, the remaining children never returned. Whereas long, cold winters, lack of supplies and equipment, wild animal attacks, black flies and disease could not defeat the Horning's Mills pioneers, this tragedy was too much. Most of them pulled up stakes and returned to safer grounds in Hamilton. Even Lewis Horning eventually abandoned his plans. At 71, he made his way back to civilization, leaving the 80 acres he'd cleared, his frame house, mills, river and dream. Six years later he sold his remaining holdings in Horning's Mills and to this day, is considered a genius by some and an eccentric by others.

The Pine River once produced power for Orangville, Shelburne and Horning's Mills.

Harnessing the Power

The promising elixir of water convinced more than one entrepreneur to set up shop at the headwaters of the Pine River high above Shelburne. But few were as resilient to life's trials as Thompson Russell (T. R.) Huxtable and his wife, Elizabeth Hunter. Their daughter, Marjorie Milroy, muses, "I never heard them complain, you know." But if anyone had reason to feel hard done by in business, it was T. R. Huxtable.

The remains of T. R. Huxtable's powerhouse, located on the Pine River a few miles downstream from town.

After completing his apprenticeship as a miller, young T. R. left his home in Horning's Mills and headed west to make his fortune. His milling skills soon landed him a job in Carmen, Manitoba. While T. R. was home for Christmas in 1897, however, his father, James, suffered an accident in the mill that required amputation of his leg. So T. R. and his brother Bob abandoned their plans to return west, electing instead to take over from their father. By 1904, the year James Huxtable died, hardworking T. R. was already looking for a new challenge. Millers' consumption had forced him to give up his work at the Huxtable Mill, but this couldn't keep him down. T. R.'s aspirations eclipsed flour milling. He envisaged turbines on the mighty Pine River producing electricity that would catapult Horning's Mills, Shelburne and their environs into the modern world.

In 1906, he approached Shelburne Town Council with his plans to build a hydro dam on the Pine. He hoped to convince them to invest in the operation and make electricity generation a municipal enterprise. An engineer hired to investigate the opportunity reported there was plenty of water power available and advised Shelburne to invest. Even Sir Adam Beck, the father of Ontario Hydro, urged Shelburne to approve the project. He assured the community that if Ontario Hydro were to run a line through the county, it would need all the electricity from the Pine River for its peak power requirements.

In 1907, the citizens of Shelburne voted on the idea. But despite all the promises and hype, they turned down the ambitious plan by a close margin of only fourteen votes.

Undeterred, T. R. approached the private sector, convincing the Dufferin Light and Power Company that his dream would work. With capitalization of $200,000 and plans to raise an additional $110,000 in a bond issue, the company was in business. As an interim measure they moved a generator from Shelburne to Horning's Mills and built a transmission line to join the power source and local communities in need of electricity.

Then, in 1909, construction of a three-turbine generator and massive dam, the largest of its kind in Ontario at the time, began. More than 100 men and 20 teams of horses worked on the project but, according to Adelaide Leitch in *Into the High County*, "Construction was plagued with labor trouble, in spite of excellent working conditions, good salaries and exceptional accommodation.... And one thing did irk them. Liquor was forbidden on the property. The men stayed just long enough to collect their first pay check and then, with monumental thirst, headed out for gayer communities. Crews were normally replaced every two weeks, but the overseers never relaxed the ban on booze."

As it turned out, failure to hold on to labourers wasn't the only problem. Bond sales were slower than expected.

Horning's Mills, looking south.

Pine River near Horning's Mills.

Soon the company's three principals had put up personal security to cover an overdraft of $45,000. Even this proved insufficient. They were forced to liquidate the Dufferin Light and Power Company and the bondholders had to spend another $46,000 to buy back their property. Rising from the rubble was the Pine River Light and Power Company, still intent on generating electricity from what remained a partially constructed dam below Horning's Mills.

Before getting on with their dream, the owners of this new energy company—T. R. Huxtable included—approached Sir Adam Beck to learn of his latest plans for Ontario Hydro. He assured them it would be ten years or more before Hydro would arrive in Dufferin County, and when it did it would purchase the locally produced electricity. Confident they would get their investment back given this promise, and, according to T. R. in his memoir *Down Memories Lane*, "have some velvet [left] over," they moved ahead with their venture.

With three years left on a franchise to supply power to Shelburne and 23 years on a similar deal with Orangeville, the future looked bright for the Pine River Light and Power Company. But how quickly conditions changed. Three short years later, "The public feeling was running in favor of Hydro all over Ontario," wrote T. R. Huxtable. "You can't keep the ocean back with a mop, the tide was coming in." The company realized it was going to lose Shelburne to Hydro, and rather than have the enterprise dismembered limb by limb, the owners suggested that Hydro buy the whole works.

Only horror can describe the response when, rather than purchasing the entire company, Hydro elected to take only the high tension lines and distribution systems in Orangeville, Shelburne and Horning's Mills. This left

Cemetery in Horning's Mills.

T. R. Huxtable, the other company principals and some 70 bondholders with a dam and powerhouse worth $100,000 and nowhere to send the electricity.

In 1922, T. R. appeared before the Hydro commission to contest the decision. Incensed at what he claims was Sir Adam Beck's about-face, T. R. asked him why he broke his promise to not enter Dufferin for at least ten years. According to T. R., Beck replied, "I didn't go in. I was invited in." Adding to T. R.'s disappointment was the fact the Pine River plant was perfectly synchronized with Hydro's needs. The revolutions per minute of the generators and the cycle phase were identical. With a simple turn of a switch, the power from the Pine River plant could have flowed into Hydro's grid.

And Dufferin paid for the decision. With the generators at Pine River silenced, the county was a long way from a source of power and forced, for a time, to pay the highest electricity rates in Southern Ontario.

Asked why he never sued Hydro, T. R. explained, "We'd have a fat chance of getting a trial with the attorney-general also a Hydro commissioner. I'd be asking him to issue an order to sue himself!"

Having lost his investment and without a livelihood, Horning's Mills' most prominent citizen moved his wife and eight children to Barrie. Hard luck followed. In Barrie, T. R. found employment driving some of Canada's earliest buses, known as jitneys. But his new career was cut short when, in 1927, the uninsured Jitney Barn burned to the ground taking its motorized occupants with it.

Unemployed once again, T. R. returned to Horning's Mills and bought property upstream from the original power plant. Shortly thereafter, in 1932, Hydro found itself without a contract with Horning's Mills. Before negotiating a new deal, Hydro had engineers evaluate the existing system. They determined Hydro needed to spend $5,000 to upgrade the transmission lines and distribution system within the village. Before it would agree to undertake these repairs, Hydro demanded the village sign a 20-year contract. Horning's Mills' trustees balked at this proposition and turned to T. R. Could he supply electricity? Delighted to oust Hydro, the indefatigable T. R. determined that he could build a new plant and distribution system for half of what Hydro said repairs would cost, and supply electricity at a lower price.

The village voted in favour of a made-at-home energy plan. Seventeen years after Hydro shut him down, T. R. was back in business. Not as grand as the original Pine River facility, the new generator nonetheless served the community well between 1932 and 1946. And it might have survived another dozen years had tragedy not struck yet again. During a rainstorm a neighbour upstream opened his dam without telling T. R. The extra water swamped his spillway and destroyed his dam. Deciding against repairs, T. R. explained his decision in his memoirs: "I had been fighting Hydro for 30 years and was getting up in years, so I did not repair the dam, but sold the property for fishing and resort purposes."

Today, the evidence of Horning's Mill's watery history is easy to find, in an old flume and the empty shell of the original power plant.

TODAY'S QUIXOTIC DREAMER

It is fitting that Horning's Mills of today has its own visionaries. Bruce Beach lives part time in a typical house on Horning's Mills' main street. His wife, Jean, centenarian mother, Violet, and several children share the house. Jean grew up in the village, but Bruce is an

All that is left of T. R. Huxtable's original powerhouse.

American; he also calls Kansas home. In that state, he built one of more than 20 nuclear fallout shelters he's been involved with across the continent.

By far his most ambitious effort, however, is on the outskirts of Horning's Mills. Here his underground nuclear shelter, called Ark II, is spread out over 10,000 square feet on property owned by his wife. He used 42 discarded buses for the shell and then surrounded them with at least 12 feet of high-strength, reinforced concrete. Another 5 to 14 feet of earth was pushed over the top. He has stocked the shelter with supplies. It has a morgue, hot water, a dentist's office, septic system and furnaces in addition to a kitchen, dormitories and other living space. He's even taken precautions so that people suffering from stress during a prolonged stay can find some relief. An immersion tank is filled with salt water. People can float effortlessly in this womb-like environment. They hear classical music, sleep and overcome their inevitable cabin fever.

Bruce gauges humanity's nearness to doomsday by the number of calls he receives from people interested in becoming members of Ark II. He explains that during the lead-up to the new millennium, interest in his shelter broke all previous records. As the phone rang, Bruce accepted new members and took up their offers of assistance. He claims, "I was not a believer in Y2K myself but I needed the help." It wasn't only helpers who showed up on Bruce's doorstep. Local authorities also began paying more attention to his activities.

He claims he's been raided by various government agencies dozens of times. A court order prevents him from taking people out to the site. He calls the situation "Waco North, Canadian-style, no guns." He puts the opposition to Ark II down to "a small country attitude" and goes on to explain, "We're Baha'i."

Though it comes as no surprise to this lugubrious builder of nuclear shelters, another event eclipsed Y2K. After the tragedy of September 11, 2001, Ark II's phone lit up once again. Bruce claims that for a time he received two or three inquiries a day, up from the two or three calls he normally fields per month.

Despite his doomsday message, Bruce's real dream is to help bring peace to the world by developing a universal language at a Universal Language Institute he hopes to build on his wife's land in Horning's Mills. A glossy brochure shows a model of a 27,000-square-metre, spaceship-like facility and blinking communication tower. Capable of accommodating 600 international students, the centre will be perched high above Horning's Mills' pine and maple forest.

Bruce Beach is the founder and builder of Ark II.

Walyngton Place, Horning's Mills.

Bruce says the area surrounding the Pine River's Little Wonder Falls that runs through the site is an old Native burial ground. Lore has it that an elder from a nearby village took his daughter to Horning's Mills and told her that great treasures of the earth would be discovered at this location. Though people have come in search of gold, silver and diamonds, they have discovered no concrete riches, lending credence to Bruce's conviction that Horning's Mills' real treasure will be its role in developing the world's first truly universal language.

The Queenston shale visible alongside the Hockley Road is a telltale sign that the Niagara Escarpment exists in Dufferin County.

In Conclusion

Poised as it is both geographically and figuratively at the edge of Toronto's urban shadow, Dufferin County is at a crossroads. So far it has largely avoided pretentious gentrification. The rich and famous who have bought up old farms in Dufferin haven't felt the need to advertise their presence with massive electronic gates. And many of Dufferin's newcomers are regular folk ready to fit in with the locals now that they have escaped the city's impersonal hustle and bustle.

Richard Proctor and his wife, Janice Calvert, typify the urban refugee. Richard writes from his home near Mansfield: "We moved to Dufferin in 1998. Apart from real estate prices and proximity to Toronto, Dufferin was attractive to us, as I'm sure it is to many people, because it provides what many 'country' settings provide: fresh air, beautiful sunsets, less traffic and noise, starry skies at night. The mix of rolling rural landscapes and small-town centres makes it a great place to live and work. So far, Dufferin is far enough away from it all to be pleasant, and close enough to make for plenty of different options."

In parts of Dufferin, agriculture still dictates the pace and texture of daily life and land is worth more for the crops it can grow than the houses it can support. Side by side with Dufferin's farmers are its artists. More and more talented painters, writers and sculptors find the big sky and dramatic landscape inspire them. Weekend retreats have become full-time homes with studios attached.

Although the differences between municipalities and among weekenders, artists, commuters, full-time farmers and business people may never be fully eliminated, Dufferin works. As long as municipal leaders allow its communities to flourish in their own unique ways, Dufferin will continue to be dearly loved by the people who live there.

For love it they do. They feel the community spirit, wonder at the same stormy skies and revel in its peace and quiet.

In the end, could it be nature that binds Dufferin together? Could its expansive vistas, picturesque rivers, deadly tornadoes, killer frosts and bogs too wet to be drained for agriculture draw the community together? Remembering the twister that devastated both his farms in 1985, Earl Dodds remarked, "You couldn't begin to cope with a disaster like that without other people."

Farm fields, Mulmur.

Orangeville's well-known Manac Moose.

Incidents such as the ice storm of 1999 remind us that nature should not be taken for granted—and that, in a fix, you need your neighbours. Just watch the phone lines light up after a good snowstorm as neighbours check in with each other.

Dan Needles, author of *Letters from Wingfield Farm*, is considered a hometown boy. He remembers his years living in Mono Township when he edited the *Shelburne Free Press & Economist*. In his own way, he comes to a similar conclusion. He writes, "But still, there was something very attractive about that community. It worked together and played together and made its own fun. It had a marvellous way of pulling together whenever there was a crisis, like a death or a fire, or a defeat in the provincial Tory party. Above all, it gave me a wonderful sense of place."

Pre-dawn in Mono.

Bibliography

Ball, Signe, ed. *In the Hills* magazine. Vol. 7, No. 1, 2000. Mono Centre, Ontario: Monolog Communications Inc., 2000.

Banks, Neil. *Laurel United Church: 100 Years in the Building, 140 Years in the Community.*

Barr, Grace, Ann Kendre and Sheila Richardson. *A Place to Pray: The Story of the Primrose United Church.* 1975.

Beaumont, Ralph. *Steam Trains to the Bruce.* Erin, Ontario: The Boston Mills Press, 1977.

Brown, Steve. *If Walls Could Talk.* Orangeville: Local Architectural Conservation Advisory Committee, 1988.

Credit Valley Conservation Authority, Department of Planning and Development. *Credit Valley Conservation Report.* 1956.

Credit Valley Conservation Foundation. *Credit River Valley.* Erin, Ontario: The Boston Mills Press, 1992.

Department of Travel and Publicity. *Pioneer Railway to be Commemorated at Orangeville.* 1960.

Dodds, Ernest, H. *Men of the Soil: A History of the Federation of Agriculture in Dufferin County and the Province of Ontario: 1942-1980.* Orangeville, Ontario: 1980.

Dufferin County Museum and Archives. *A Celebration of 50 Years of the Canadian Fiddlers Open Old Time Fiddle Championship: 1951–2000.* 2000.

Dufferin County, Ontario: The Corporation of the County of Dufferin, 1975.

"Footpaths to Freeways: The Story of Ontario's Roads, Ontario's Bicentennial 1784-1984."

Graham, Esther. *One Hundred Years Along the Upper Grand: 1881–1981: A History of East Luther Township.*

Grand River Conservation Authority and the Ontario Ministry of Natural Resources. *Luther Marsh Management Plan.* 1991.

Halbert, Mabel L. *Memories of an Old Cog.* 1980.

Heyes, Esther. *The Story of Albion.* Bolton, Ontario: The Bolton Enterprise, 1961.

Huxtable, Thompson Russell. *Down Memories Lane, 1875–1959.* Shelburne Free Press and Economist Print, 1959.

Kelling, Elizabeth Anne. *The Roots of Amaranth.* Erin, Ontario: The Boston Mills Press, 1981.

Keough, Pat & Rosemarie. *The Niagara Escarpment, A Profile.* Ontario: A Stoddart/Nahanni Production, 1990.

Ketchum, Jesse. *Jesse Ketchum Diary: 1859-1860.*

Kosydar, Richard. *Natural Landscapes of the Niagara Escarpment.* Dundas, Ontario: Tiereron Press, 1996.

Labatt, Lori and Bruce Littlejohn. *Islands of Hope.* Willowdale, Ontario: Firefly Books Ltd., 1992.

Leitch, Adelaide. *Into the High County: The Story of Dufferin, The Last 12,000 Years to 1974.*

McWhirter, G. R. *The Keldon Folk.* 1925.

Marshall, John Ewing. *Fifty Years of Rural Life in Dufferin County.*

——. *Half Century of Farming in Dufferin.*

——. *St. Andrew's United Church: A Century of Service.* Camilla.

Marsville W. I. *Tweedsmuir Village History, 1905-1947.*

McKitrick, A. M. *Steam Trains Through Orangeville.* Erin, Ontario: The Boston Mills Press, 1976.

Mulmur Historical Committee. *Mulmur, The Story of a Township.* 1951.

Pearson, Lester B. *Mike, The Memories of the Right Honourable, Volume 1.* New American Library, 1972.

Porter, Ina, ed. *Orangeville Centennial 100 Years: An Historical Review of the Town of Orangeville, 1863–1963.*

Read, Allan. *Unto The Hills: A History of the Parish of East Mono.* 1952.

Relessey Cemetery Board. *History Relessey United Church: 1870-1970.* 1971.

Richardson, William G. *The Story of Whittington: A History of the Whittington Community of Dufferin County.*

Rose, John. *History of Shelburne.*

Ross, Nicola and Gord Handley. *Caledon.* Erin, Ontario: The Boston Mills Press, 1999.

St. Mark's Anglican Church, Orangeville, Ontario. *History: 1837-1967.*

Sawden, Stephen. *History of Dufferin County.*

Shortt, Ioan & Elmer. *Monticello United Church: 100 Years of Devotion: 1883–1983.*

Slater, Patrick (John W. Mitchell). *The Yellow Briar.* MacMillan Co. of Canada. 1933.

St. Andrew's Presbyterian Church, Mansfield, Ontario, 125th Anniversary: 1863–1988.

The History of the Parish of Orangeville: 1876-1976.

The Story of Orangeism: Its Origin and History of a Century and a Quarter in Canada, particularly Ontario West. [more?]

Theberg, John, B. *Legacy: The Natural History of Ontario.* Toronto, Ontario: McClelland & Stewart Inc., 1989.

Thompson, Russel B. *Elder and the Pioneers.*

Tovell, Walter, M. *Guide to the Geology of the Niagara Escarpment.* Ontario: The Niagara Escarpment Commission. 1992.

Trout, J. M. & Edward. *The Railways of Canada.* Toronto: Coles Canada Collection, 1970.

Turnbull, Jean. *Still Burns Their Flame: The 150 Year History of Burns Church,* Mono Centre. 1988.

Willmot, Elizabeth. *Meet Me at the Station.* McBain Publications, Inc., 1976.

Index of Place Names

Black Bank 21, 23, 24

Bowling Green 92, 102

Camilla 9, 11, 38, 46

Corbetton 12, 40, 111

Crombie's Station 55

Fraxa 53, 55, 56, 61

Gooseville 11, 114

Grand Valley 25, 28, 37, 45, 56, 59, 78, 79, 81, 94, 97–99, 107

Hockley Valley 11, 14, 24, 59, 87, 108

Honeywood 21, 83, 85, 91, 93

Horning's Mills 20, 25, 119, 121, 123–126, 128, 129

Kilgorie 23

Laurel 38, 40, 55

Lavender 19, 23

Mansfield 19, 37, 38, 42, 116, 131

The Maples 65

Mono Centre 13, 19, 23, 58

Mono Mills 19, 36, 38, 40, 45, 59, 75

Monticello 16, 30, 38, 111

Orangeville 11, 12, 14–16, 23–26, 36–38, 40, 43, 45, 49, 50–53, 55–57, 59, 60–63, 65–70, 72, 73, 75, 76, 78, 79, 94, 96, 97, 99, 105, 107–109, 114, 119, 124, 132

Primrose 20, 21, 38, 46, 62

Purple Hill 36, 43, 72

Redickville 15, 35

Relessey 38, 39, 46

Rosemont 21, 38, 42, 61, 63, 69

Shelburne 11, 12, 14, 20, 25, 35, 37, 38, 40, 46, 51–53, 55, 67, 69, 70, 75–78, 87, 88, 91, 92, 94, 97, 102, 105–107, 111, 113–115, 119, 121, 123, 124

Stanton 36, 42, 81

Violet Hill 20, 21, 23, 36, 74

Waldemar 37, 56, 59

Whitfield 46

Whittington 38, 85, 87